THE FALL OF THE
IDOLS

THE FALL OF THE IDOLS

by

WILLIAM RALPH INGE
Formerly Dean of St Paul's

PUTNAM · LONDON
42 GREAT RUSSELL STREET, W.C. 1

First Published October 1940
Reprinted December 1940

As for myself, the recognition that we are living in
a more brutal age than that, say, of Elizabeth, does
not inspire one to write hopeful poetry or even con-
jectural prose, but simply makes one sit still in an
apathy and watch the clock spinning backwards with
a wonder if, when it gets back to the Dark Ages and
the sack of Rome, it will ever move forward again to
a new Renascence and a new literature. But people
would call this pessimistic, so I will stop.

— Thomas Hardy in 1914

To suffer woes which Hope thinks infinite;
To forgive wrongs darker than death or night;
  To defy Power which seems omnipotent;
To love, to bear; to hope till Hope creates
From its own wreck the thing it contemplates;
  Neither to change nor falter nor repent;
This, like thy glory, Titan, is to be
Good, great and joyous, beautiful and free;
This is alone Life, Joy, Empire, and Victory.

— Shelley, *Prometheus Unbound*

CONTENTS

INTRODUCTION

Like most old men whose lives have been prolonged beyond the Psalmist's span, I wish that my call to rest had come before the outbreak of this hideous and suicidal war. At the time of writing, the course of the struggle, and the date of its termination, are quite uncertain, and I can offer no prediction. But whether the war ends in a stalemate or in an admission of failure by either side, a heavy blow has been struck at European civilisation in the next half-century. The Great War which began in 1914 was like the first stroke which often warns a man that he has been living imprudently and that his life is in danger. The warning was disregarded, and the second stroke has come. The England into which I was born eighty years ago, the England which I have known and loved, will be completely changed. Our position as a world-power had long been precarious, and, as many good judges have pointed out, there could be no recovery for

9

our island empire after a decisive defeat. The United States and Russia are almost invulnerable; France and Germany have shown that they can be as strong as ever a few years after a shattering defeat; but we should not recover. Even if we escape defeat, we shall be too much impoverished to maintain a fleet as powerful as that of America. The sea-power will cross the Atlantic. We shall join the *ci-devant* Great Powers— Spain, Holland and Sweden.

At home, almost everything that my upbringing has led me to prize will be doomed. The English country house, the fine flower of our civilisation and one of the few beautiful things which we have to show to the foreigner, will disappear. Our public schools, which with all their faults have kept up a great tradition in our national character, will fight a losing battle and eventually succumb. The scholar and scientist with independent means, to whose activities our country owes much of its fame in literature, learning and research, may have to make way for the professional lecturer and populariser. In these and other ways the war will break our old traditions. I am thankful that

10

I shall not have to live in the England of the near future.

There is of course no reason why intellectually and spiritually we should not continue to make great contributions to the true wealth of humanity. If we do, we shall receive much more sympathy and admiration from foreign nations than when our rather blatant prosperity made us disliked even more than envied. The time may come when history will endorse the judgment of our kindly American critic George Santayana. The Englishman 'carries his English weather in his heart wherever he goes; it becomes a cool spot in the desert, and a steady and sane oracle amongst all the deliriums of mankind. Never since the heroic days of Greece has the world had such a sweet, just, boyish master. It will be a black day for the human race when scientific blackguards, conspirators, churls, and fanatics manage to supplant him.'

It would not be a happy or a peaceful world which would follow a German victory over the British Commonwealth. 'When the oak falls', says a Greek proverb, 'every man gathers faggots.' If the United States of

11

Europe ever comes into being, it will be by agreement, not by conquest. Napoleon at St. Helena professed that such a league of nations was in his mind, but it was not. This super-brigand awakened the dormant spirit of nationality which ruined him, and this spirit is far stronger now than it was a century and a half ago, when Germany and Italy were little more than geographical expressions. The conquests of the Directory were made under the inspiring slogan, 'Liberty, equality and fraternity', addressed to nations which enjoyed none of them. French civilisation has a superficial attractiveness which makes the idea of French domination less odious to other nations than subjection to any other foreign power. Germany has nothing of the kind to offer. The character which Livy unfairly ascribes to Hannibal—*inhumana crudelitas, perfidia plus quam Punica*—sums up all that the world sees in Hitlerian Germany. The second Napoleonic empire cannot be of long duration.

But the events of the last few months have undoubtedly given a new complexion to the international situation. Last winter the late Warden of New College, H. A. L. Fisher,

the eminent historian and former Cabinet
Minister, was lunching at our house. I said
to him, 'Is it wise for our Ministers to make
speeches which seem to shut the doors upon
any possible peace by agreement? Do we
want to convince the Germans that they are
fighting not for the domination of Europe
but for their national existence?' To my
amazement he answered, 'It is the French.
They are determined to *dismember* Germany
this time.' And now the French, who in
1870, after the destruction of their armies,
defended Paris heroically and without hope
of success, the French, whose 'Ils ne pas-
seront pas' won the admiration of the whole
world in the Great War, are sitting down
quietly under such a humiliation as has seldom before overtaken a great nation. We
are told that their politics are so corrupt that
they do not think the Third Republic worth
fighting for. The Right Wing favours some
authoritarian government: the Communists
opposed the war from the first. The same
collapse has occurred in other countries. The
shameful treachery of Leopold of Belgium
has not made him unpopular with his subjects. Norway, Denmark, even Holland, that

13

group of free countries which in their history have shown a fine spirit of independence, have submitted with suspicious readiness. We have heard a great deal of German propaganda, of 'Fifth Columns' and bribes; but it is plain that in all these nations there is a large section which has chosen surrender rather than fight to the last for the independence of their native lands.

This attitude has been a complete surprise to almost everyone in this country. We have laughed at the British Fascists, but even in England there are disloyal brains behind a foolish and well-meaning movement. There is something more than aggressive nationalism in the totalitarian attack upon the West, something, it may be, stronger than the love of liberty itself.

Is this the beginning of a new series of wars of religion? Are the 'ideas of 1789', which swept the world in the nineteenth century, now fighting a losing battle against a revival of the old régime in a harsher and more scientific form? Or should we find a closer parallel in the early conquests of Islam, or even in Genghiz Khan, who overran Europe and Asia from Kieff to Pekin?

The 'New Order', of which Germans and Italians are already speaking, has borrowed much from syndicalism, while repudiating the idea of class-warfare. This may be a valuable experiment. It has frankly adopted a grinding and all-pervasive tyranny. It preaches a fanatical worship of the State, and hatred of other nations. There can be no peace between nationalism and internationalism; the latter must arm itself with a better ideology than the discredited Marxian propaganda. I cannot even guess what is likely to happen, but the present state of Europe is mere co-operative suicide.

The terrible catastrophe of last September made me doubt whether it was worth while to write this book. A post-mortem diagnosis is not very interesting. But my conclusion, after reading the opinions of the multitude of amateur physicians who have pronounced that one of the great cycles of human history has come to an end, and that we are embarking on an unknown and uncharted sea, is that though the idols of the nineteenth century are indeed broken and dishonoured, there are older traditions—Christianity, humanism, liberty and science—which have not been broken, though 'the acids of modernity' have eaten into the surface of all of them. From Spengler to H. G. Wells I think the force of tradition, the continuity of history, has been underestimated. Even in the great crises of history, such as the fall of the West Roman Empire and the end of the middle ages, the break with the past was far from complete, and I do not think that present conditions herald any changes so subversive as the barbarisation of Europe in the fifth century or the end of Church-directed civilisation at the Renaissance and Reformation. Events which at the time, and long afterwards, seemed to have changed the whole face of the world, are now seen to have been local and transitory storms. The French Revolution which, like most revolutions, took place on a rising market, the result of aspiration rather than desperation, was the work of a comparatively small gang who took advantage of the bankruptcy of a 'benevolent despotism', and the career of Napoleon might be plausibly represented as a gigantic irrelevance. Neither of them hindered the development of middle-class ascendancy which industrialism had made

16

inevitable. A pendulum too violently agitated springs back vigorously. Revolutions may register a change in the balance of power; they seldom effect anything permanent.

To those who have been brought up in the unquestioning worship of nineteenth century fetishes—Progress, Democracy, Free Trade, Socialism—it must be a shock to see those venerable idols shaking on their pedestals or lying prostrate at the foot of them. Such a state of things gives ample room for discussion. But these changes have come about gradually, and the war may only hasten developments which were inevitable without it. I hope therefore that even if this book appears when the nation is rent by bitter anxiety, it may find a few readers who will look in it, certainly not for prophecy, for I see no vision, but perhaps for some indication of the direction which European affairs are likely to take after peace has been restored. For unquestionably the young are in revolt against all the traditions of their elders. They will not always be young, and they will not always be revolutionary; but the bands of authority have been loosened as never before, and every tradition must now justify itself before a sceptical and impatient tribunal.

W. R. I.

BRIGHTWELL MANOR
September 1940

I
PROGRESS

I

PROGRESS

Wordsworth says that we live by admiration, hope and love, and that as
these are rightly blended, and fixed on the
right objects, we ascend in dignity of being.
We are concerned in this chapter with the
second of these—Hope. The last century has
been called the century of hope, and hopefulness in that period was centred on what
was called progress, that is, changes in
society, and perhaps in the units who consti-
tute society, towards conditions which were
thought or assumed to be more desirable
than their past and present states. Belief in
this progress was the lay religion of the last
century, and the decline of this belief has
had a profound effect on the whole outlook
of our contemporaries. Of all the idols which
our grandparents worshipped, this is the one
whose downfall has been most disturbing to
the faith of those who are detached from
Christian tradition.

Although Christianity gave the world a

new triad of moral virtues in place of the four cardinal virtues of Paganism, and placed Hope as the second of them, between Faith and Love, it cannot be said that the belief in a law of mundane progress was brought into the world by Christianity. It is indeed a comparatively recent thing, and it is to a large extent a substitute for the other-worldly hope which the Church had fostered, but which has faded noticeably in modern times. Belief in a law of progress, it has been said, is the last great Western heresy.

St. Paul says truly that the Jews against hope believed in hope. No nation ever suffered such cruel disappointments; but they would not give up their belief that somehow and somewhen justice is done in this world. 'Shall not the Judge of all the earth do right?' is the question asked in the Book of Genesis, and the whole of the Old Testament is full of attempts to justify the ways of God to man. Every conceivable explanation of the evil in the world is tried in turn. The sins of the fathers are visited on the children; the apparently righteous sufferer is a secret sinner; the nation, not the individual, is the unit; vicarious suffering is the law of re-

22

demption; and at last, strangely late in their history, a new world is called into existence to redress the balance of the old. To some extent history has justified their indomitable faith. The Jews have stood by the graves of all their oppressors in turn. They may yet say to their latest persecutor: 'The feet of them that buried Assyrians, Babylonians, Greeks, Romans, and Spanish Inquisitors are at the door, and shall carry thee out.' But, as the writer to the Hebrews says, the heroes of the old dispensation received not the promise, nor was it ever fulfilled as they hoped and expected. Hope must die to live. No pure hope shall wither, except that a purer may spring out of its roots. But when God 'provided some better thing', the obstinate nationalism of Israel would not accept it. This has been the tragedy of a noble race.

Judaism, then, was a religion of hope, but not a religion of progress in the modern sense. It contained elements which prevented Christianity from being a purely other-worldly or acosmistic religion, like Hinduism. Belief in a law of progress may, just possibly, be traced back in part to this

23

earlier religion of hope; but other influences were more potent.

Still less can we find traces of a belief in progress in Graeco-Roman Paganism. No one before Christ made hope a moral virtue. To the Pagans it was a gift of doubtful value, an illusion which helps us to endure life, and a valuable spur to action; but on the whole a will of the wisp. Very characteristic is the Greek epigram which that modern Pagan, Lord Brougham, inscribed on his villa at Cannes:

> *I've entered port. Fortune and Hope adieu;*
> *Make game of others, for I've done with*
> *you.*[1]

St. Paul was justified in saying that the Pagans of his time 'had no hope'. The literature even of the Augustan age is full of such despairing utterances as Horace's well-known stanza, beginning '*Damnosa quid non imminuit dies?*' Time was the enemy, not the friend of man. Civilisation, outwardly so prosperous, was already inwardly beginning

---

[1] The Greek epigram is:

ἐλπὶς καὶ σὺ τύχη μέγα χαίρετε · τὸν λιμέν' εὗρον·
οὐδὲν ἐμοὶ χ' ὑμῖν, παίζετε τοὺς μετ' ἐμέ.

to wither. '*In cordibus aruerat*', as Gregory the Great says: in men's hearts it had dried up. This is very apparent in Seneca, Lucan, and afterwards in Tacitus, who finds it plain that the gods have no care for our happiness, but only for our punishment. As early as Lucretius we have the complaint that the soil is exhausted. This was probably true; unscientific farming and the destructive goat contributed to the desiccation of the Mediterranean lands. In the third century a chorus of woe proceeds from Pagans and Christians alike. But by this time pessimism was only too well justified.

Aeschylus and Euripides both knew that the human race has advanced from savagery. But the golden age, for all the ancients, was in the past, not in the near future. Life in the golden age was certainly simpler, but it was happier. The prevailing view was not that mankind at first lived in paradise, but that the history of the universe is one of alternate progress and decline. They had happened on a period of decline. This is the famous theory of cycles, of which we have certainly not heard the last, though most modern writers, including even J. B. Bury and philosophic historians like Arnold Toyn-bee,[1] reject it with indignation as absolute pessimism. Why it should be called pessimistic it is not easy to see, unless we condemn the time and place we live in as the worst of all possible worlds. Even our astronomers, Jeans and Eddington, are manifestly prejudiced against the idea of recurrence, and are glad that they can find no recuperative principle in nature. On this more must be said presently. The theory of cycles has been favoured by Origen, and in modern times by Machiavelli, Goethe, Shelley, Nietzsche, and the astronomer Arrhenius. Einstein a few years ago was inclined to be-

[1] *A Study of History*, iv, pp. 30–34. We should be 'the victims of an everlasting cosmic practical joke'. 'All human endurance becomes the torment of a Tityos or an Ixion.' This is an extraordinary notion. Professor Toynbee thinks that there is 'manifestly a progress towards an end'. It is not at all manifest, or rather it is manifest that the end must be the extinction of all life on this planet. An infinite purpose, if such a thing were possible, would be eternally frustrate. God has many finite purposes, a few of which are bound up with our little lives. When these are finished, we can say 'Now lettest Thou Thy servant depart in peace', knowing that our lives in time are the sacrament of timeless reality. 'Nothing that *is* can ever perish', as Plotinus says. To throw our ideals into the future, Bosanquet says, is the death of all sane idealism. The future, Anatole France tells us, is a convenient place in which to store our dreams.

lieve in a vast pulsation of the universe, as opposed to the prevalent view that all ponderable matter is in flight from the centre. Science has not yet said its last word on this subject.

Plato believed in a 'great year', a cosmic cycle, perhaps of 72,000 years. Aristotle thought that the arts and sciences have been discovered and lost 'an infinite number of times'. The Pythagoreans and Stoics even believed that there will be an exact repetition of events. Marcus Aurelius says that an intelligent man of forty may be said to have seen all that has happened or ever will happen.

The Epicureans did not believe in cycles, and Lucretius is the first to use the word progress (*pedetentim progredientes*); but they knew that the world is ultimately doomed to destruction. In sonorous lines which were evidently famous in antiquity Lucretius says:

'*Principio maria et terras caelumque tuere ;*
quorum naturam triplicem, tria corpora,
     Memmi,
tres species tam dissimiles, tria talia texta,
una dies dabit exitio, multosque per annos
sustentata ruet moles et machina mundi.'

The belated champions of a law of progress often fail to distinguish between progress as a law of nature and progress as a fact of history. They sometimes suppose that those who deny the law also deny the fact. They ought to distinguish between a study of history since the beginning of civilisation and a metaphysical theory which makes progress a cosmic principle. The latter theory became popular in the eighteenth century, and we may hope that it will die in the twentieth. It had an early advocate in Leibniz, who has been called the father of optimism. The universe is the best of all possible worlds, not necessarily for humanity, but for the cosmos as a whole. Rather inconsistently he thinks that this best of all possible worlds will become more and more perfect through infinite time. This opinion, since no reasons are or can be given for it, must be temperamental: wishful thinking, to use a modern phrase.

Bacon had already fallen a victim to the misleading parallel between the life of an individual, ending in senile decay, and the course of a civilisation. Something like this theory seems to survive in Spengler, Christopher Dawson, and others. There is no apparent reason why a civilisation should grow old like a man; but it must be owned that in history civilisations have passed their prime and declined. The causes have been very various—biological retrogression, aided by wars and sanguinary civic broils, or by a cacogenic birth-rate; foreign conquest; 'loss of nerve', as Gilbert Murray puts it, a *taedium vitae* which has certainly overtaken some nations and is even now depopulating some of the South Sea islands; bad governments, such as Turkish misrule, and in earlier times the inflation policy of the Roman mint. But no law limiting the life of a civilisation to so many centuries can be based on these widely different causes of decline and fall.

Rousseau, an optimist on human nature and a pessimist on civilisation, has been one of the most noxious influences that history records. Gibbon, speaking without much conviction, allows us to 'acquiesce in the pleasing conclusion that every age of the world has increased and still increases the real wealth, the happiness, the knowledge and perhaps the virtue of the human race'.

29

With Priestley we come to the romantic or apocalyptic dreams which were to carry the writers of the nineteenth century far beyond the bounds of reason. 'Whatever was the beginning of this world, the end will be glorious and paradisaical beyond what our imaginations can now conceive'. Condorcet in France and Godwin in England preached the perfectibility of man, a dogma supported only by an *a priori* view of human nature.[1] The fury of such men when Malthus published his cold douche may be imagined. The Lake poets were captivated by Godwin, but soon recovered their equilibrium; Wordsworth recanted his 'proud and most presumptuous confidence'.

The fanatics of perfectibility fall into two classes. On the one side there are the Utopians who resemble the chiliasts or millenarians of early Christianity. For them the beneficent revolution is to occur catastrophically in the near future. The bad institutions to which they attribute the corruption of innocent human nature are to be abolished. The last king, as Shelley gracefully said, is to be

[1] More examples will be found in Acton's *Lectures on Modern History*, pp. 324–5.

strangled in the entrails of the last priest. Then the world will be an earthly paradise, and men will live in a state of immobile perfection. No further change need be looked for: the redemption of humanity from sin and misery will have been accomplished. This is the creed of revolutionary socialism or communism, which has inspired all the Utopians from Sir Thomas More to our own day. It is significant that the older Utopias are placed in some distant part of the world, while the later are to be in Europe, but at a future date. The other school looks for a slow and gradual amelioration, which will proceed for endless aeons, till perfection is reached. This was the dream of nineteenth century Liberalism.

The apostolate of perfectibility next passed into the hands of German philosophers. Herder, a deist of what I have called the second school, holds that by the constitution imposed upon creation by the original fiat of the Creator, 'the flower of humanity, captive still in its germ, will blossom out into the true form of man like God, in a state of which we cannot imagine the greatness and majesty.'

31

Kant believes in final causes, and argues that if final causes can be traced in particular instances, there must be one final purpose in the whole. This entirely unjustifiable inference had a great effect on nineteenth century theology. But he is much more cautious than other thinkers about the certainty of progress. He is content to find that there has in fact been progress in the past, and thinks it probable that there will be further progress in the future. He is also emphatic that by progress he does not mean an increase of happiness. For him there is nothing good except the good will.

Fichte pays small regard to history, since he insists that his theses are already proved independently of history. The progress of the race, which he regards as certain, will be based on knowledge of the eternal truths of reason.

Hegel assigns a far greater value to history than Fichte, but like most of his contemporaries he exaggerates the importance of political and institutional forms. Lutheranism has always tended to deify the State, and to separate public from private morality. In Hegel the State is almost an incarnation of the divine Spirit, which has already attained self-consciousness in 'the German spirit, which is the spirit of the modern world'. He has no clear vision of any further progress.

Goethe was too cool-headed to be carried away by any apocalyptic dreams. History may run for thousands or even for millions of years. But men will not become better or happier, except for limited periods. 'The time will come when the Creator will become tired of us men, and another cycle will then begin. Meanwhile, we can enjoy ourselves on this dear old playground.'

The French Revolution was in part caused by the philosophers of perfectibility, especially the disciples of Rousseau. The failure of their fantastic promises naturally alienated many who had begun by welcoming the revolution. Guizot, however, though he admitted that 'la Providence a ses aises dans le temps', as St. Bernard had said '*habet mundus iste noctes suas et non paucas*', found in history a slow but unquestionable process of amelioration, which gives ground to expect a long vista of gradual progress in the future.

Fourier with his 'phalansteries' and predictions of a time when sharks and tigers will become tame and friendly to man is hardly worth noticing, though at the time many took him seriously. Comte's famous three stages do not really fit even European history, much less the history of the world. The Vatican by this time had begun to be frightened, and in 1864 appeared the startling *Syllabus Errorum*, which ends by declaring that the Pope 'cannot reconcile himself with progress, liberalism, and modern civilisation'. Was this thunderbolt absurdly reactionary, or prescient of a time when the idols of the nineteenth century would be thrown from their pedestals?

In our own country the generation after the Napoleonic War was not a happy one. There was much distress, with one or two false dawns of prosperity, and fears of revolution, just as there were after the Great War. Public men were for the most part pessimistic; Wellington in the last year of his life thanked God that he would not live to see the ruin which was coming upon England. These false predictions, mostly pessimistic, are so interesting that a few more examples may be given, some of them of a rather earlier date. Shelburne: 'When Ame-

34

rica gains independence, the sun of England will set, and her glories be eclipsed for ever.' Burke in 1790: 'France does not exist politically; it is expunged out of the map of Europe.' In 1793 he thought that France might be partitioned like Poland. Wellington in 1832: 'Few people will be sanguine enough to imagine that we shall ever again be as prosperous as we have been.' Napoleon: 'Europe will be either republican or Cossack.' William Wilberforce: 'I dare not marry; the future is so unsettled.' Shaftesbury in 1848: 'Nothing can save the British Empire from shipwreck.' Disraeli in 1847: 'In industry, commerce and agriculture there is no hope.' The politician has the myopic prescience of a stockbroker. If he were not short-sighted he would be lost. Men of letters sometimes see more clearly, as when Heine said to the French: 'You have more to fear from liberated Germany than from the whole Holy Alliance.' So Matthew Arnold and George Meredith foresaw the German peril, while Sir Charles Dilke omitted Germany from the great nations of the future.

The early Victorians did not foretell the

burst of unexampled prosperity which began about 1850. This prosperity was not welcomed by men like Ruskin and Matthew Arnold, but the general hopefulness and confidence found expression in Macaulay's history. For the idea of progress had now come to England, and was acclaimed with almost blatant confidence by men of science. Herbert Spencer believed not only in progress but in perfectibility. 'Progress is not an accident but a necessity. What we call evil and immorality must disappear. It is certain that man must become perfect.' 'Always towards perfection is the mighty movement—towards a complete development and a more unmixed good.'

It was commonly supposed that this queer superstition, far more baseless than any religious dogma, was countenanced by Darwin's theory of evolution. Nothing could be further from the truth. Darwin himself believed in the fact of progress, but he had no wish to see his discoveries taken out of their context and made into laws for the universe. Darwinism includes no valuation. Its only criterion is the success of whatever happens to survive, without any regard for its character. The doctrine that what is strongest must be best, and that ideas which are generally accepted must be right, has no scientific justification. 'It dominates our minds', says Bradley 'to an extent of which most of us are perhaps dangerously unaware.' I have quoted elsewhere grotesque paeans of optimism by J. B. Crozier and the Italian philosopher Croce. It is indeed strange that this superstition, which seemed to be almost extinct, has been revived in all its absurdity by the Italian new idealists, Croce and Gentile.

The nineteenth century scientists were not idealists like Hegel, but mechanicists, who in their studies were to all intents and purposes materialists. They did not realise that mechanism and evolution are contradictory concepts. One asserts quantitative permanence and the determinism of natural law, the other qualitative transformation and the genesis of individual forms.

Another blunder was to identify progress with increased complexity, which is often a false step in evolution. Man is less specialised than the anthropoid apes.

The theory of progress as a cosmic law

labours under the unusual disability that unlike most philosophical theories it can be
definitely disproved. It is both metaphysi-
cally self-contradictory and scientifically impossible. It is strange to read even in Samuel
Alexander that 'the universe is a growing
universe, and is through and through historical.' Apart from the central position
which this theory gives to the time-process,
which most philosophers have refused to
admit as ultimately real, there can be no
growth or development in the macrocosm.
The all cannot grow or change. But it does
not necessarily follow that Bradley is right
when he says, 'as regions of mere fact and
event, the bringing into being and the
maintenance of temporal existence, our
world and every other possible world have
no value.' These words approach the acosmistic philosophy of India.

Since philosophers are not agreed on what
seems to me obvious, it would be a mistake
to lay great stress on metaphysical objections. On the scientific side there can be no
question that the law of endless progress is
bankrupt. We might have thought it incredible that any intelligent man should try

to erect into a cosmic principle the local and temporary adjustments to a changing environment which have taken place during a few thousand years among some societies of a single species on one small planet. But the wish to believe is not often recognised as a reason to doubt, and men of science are by no means exempt from popular prejudices.

The Second Law of Thermodynamics, which the French call the principle of Carnot, and which is often known as the principle of (increasing) entropy, is no new discovery. Briefly it gives us a one-way road leading to the death of the universe. The whole cosmos is steadily running down like a clock. When the process is complete, at some distant date which we could name if we knew it, there will be no more life or motion anywhere. Either matter will be 'annihilated' by the coalescence of electrons and protons neutralising each other—a notion which since the discovery of neutrons seems to be on the way to be abandoned—or there will be nothing left except incombustible ash. All the works of man and the memory of them will be as if they had never been. Even those who see objections to accepting this law of the degradation of energy as a universal principle can have no doubt that a time will come when our earth will be, like the moon, a dead world no longer habitable. The prophecy of Lucretius, and of Psalm 102, will most certainly be fulfilled. And therewith, beyond a peradventure, disappears the doctrine of the never-ending progress of humanity.

The reluctance to see the significance of entropy does not seem to have been due to doubts about the truth of the theory. But although physicists like Eddington tell us that anyone who doubts it puts himself out of court at once, there are difficulties which do not seem to have been entirely overcome. In the first place, though all mathematical calculations are theoretically reversible, the degradation of energy is said to be irreversible. For the mathematician time is of no importance;[1] for the physicist, if entropy is true, it is the supreme reality. Thus this law seems to introduce an exception, an irregularity, into the scheme of things. Analogy

[1] And yet Sir James Jeans thinks that God is a mathematician. If He is, my chances of salvation are, I fear, small. How does one pray to a mathematical God? 'O x^n, have mercy upon us!'

would lead us to expect that by the side of the destructive forces which are slowly bringing about the final death of the universe, there must be other forces which build up matter, so that an equilibrium is preserved. Some scientists, including Professor Millikan, have tried to find such agencies, for instance in the newly discovered cosmic rays; but in the opinion of most of the small number who are entitled to speak, they have not succeeded. The question, however, cannot be said to be closed.

The acceptance of entropy also raises an insoluble difficulty about the beginning of the process. As no agency can be imagined which produced the very strange state of things when entropy was at a minimum, the natural conclusion would be that the universe 'started with a bang', as Eddington says. This he quite rightly refuses to believe, though he can see no alternative. It seems to me that this impasse should make our authorities very slow to accept entropy as a universal law. It is not a case where they have a right to acquiesce in ignorance. For the only possibility, if the one-way road to destruction is an established fact, is a sudden creation out of nothing, in time. Traditional orthodoxy favours both the creation of the universe in time and its destruction in time; but the modern Christian philosopher would not find the 'start with a bang' much more acceptable than the scientist does. Even St. Thomas Aquinas jibbed at creation in time, though he thought himself obliged to accept it as revealed truth.

The question can be discussed only in connection with the terrible metaphysical problem of the status of time in reality, into which I cannot enter here. But the physicists whom I have mentioned show a tendency to take refuge in Berkeleyan idealism, a line of retreat which I think is barred to them.[1] It is a singular fact that astronomers and physicists are usually theists, while biologists are often materialists. But astronomy and physics, like all the natural sciences, begin with concrete objects—such as stars and atoms—regarded as real. Their studies

[1] Professor Levy (*The Universe of Science*, p. vi) says, 'The interpreters of the new knowledge have almost without exception approached their problems against a background of outworn idealistic philosophy.' The great Max Planck is surely right when he says, 'A science that starts off by denying its objectivity has already passed sentence on itself.'

42

are soon carried far beyond what our un-
aided senses can perceive, and their re-
searches seem to depend more and more on
mathematics, which deal with hypothetical
entities. But to begin with stars and atoms
and end with pure mentalism seems to me to
involve a *salto mortale* which reason refuses
to sanction. It is as illegitimate as the argument too often used by half-educated apologists for religion, that since matter has been
proved to consist not of minute solid billiard
balls, but of electrical charges, materialism
has been once for all disproved.

If we discard the utterly untenable notion
of progress continued to infinity, we may
fairly say that the Second Law of Thermodynamics does not concern us in any practical way. For scientists are agreed in giving
us so long a lease of this planet that the
human race, or at least the civilised part of it,
may be still in its infancy, at the stage of the
rattle and feeding-bottle. So far as I can
gather, there are only two possibilities which
might curtail our tenancy, apart from the
suggestion that our wars may end in mutual
extermination. A wandering star may approach too near our sun, as according to one

theory it did once when it gave birth to our planetary system, or the sun may blow up and become a Nova, a fate which has befallen many stars within the range of our telescopes. Both are said to be exceedingly improbable.

We may therefore leave these astronomical problems, though I must confess that I hanker after the old theory of cosmic cycles. It seems to me that if time is the moving image of eternity, the time-form of eternity is perpetuity. All Platonists must wish that this may be the truth. Whittaker even says that if entropy were established as an universal law, the whole scheme of the later Platonists would be upset. I doubt whether this necessarily follows, but certainly an infinite series of finite purposes, each with its beginning, middle, and end, is more consonant with this philosophy than the irrevocable doom which is accepted so complacently by Jeans and Eddington.

It is only natural that many Christians have tried to prove, or rather have assumed without evidence, that this lay religion of the nineteenth century is also a doctrine of Christianity, which, they say, assures us of the ultimate triumph of the Gospel. The attempt is quite futile. No religious teacher, even Buddha, has ever been so open as Jesus Christ in predicting that His doctrine would never be accepted by the majority. The Gospels are full of such sayings as 'if they have persecuted me, they will also persecute you; if they have kept my saying, they will keep yours also'. 'When the Son of Man cometh, shall he find faith on the earth?' The early Church, and the medieval Church, never thought of such a thing as a law of progress. 'The world is very evil, The times are waxing late.' The era of the Church militant, they thought, is drawing to a close; the Church triumphant will have said good-bye to this earth. Millenarianism, which broke out sporadically, was characteristic of the sect-type, not of the great Church.

Another doctrine, based on the prevalent belief in human perfectibility, was that of progress in a future life. Give the soul, said Tennyson, the wages of going on and not to die. Browning says: 'And I shall thereupon Take rest ere I begone Once more on my adventure brave and new.' Browning believed in reincarnation, Tennyson in survival in time. It is obvious that belief in unending progress after death depends on converting eternity into an endless series of moments of time, snipped off at one end but not at the other. In eternity, as a timeless state, there can be fruition or torment, but no progress, and this is the traditional Christian doctrine. The only concession to the notion that spirits will be subject to time after death is the Roman Catholic doctrine of purgatory, which is not, as many Protestants believe, a 'second paper' to decide the fate of those who are near the border-line, but a period of purification for those who are to be saved, but are not yet fit for heaven. The doctrine satisfies our sense of justice, but nothing has been revealed, and perhaps no revelation on such a subject would be possible. We should recognise that such questions as whether we should be bored in heaven, and whether eternal punishment is consistent with the character of God, are meaningless if we believe that, as the Apocalypse says, in the eternal world 'there shall be time no longer'.

We may now dismiss the alleged law of progress as a superstition unsupported either by science or religion. It is quite another question whether progress is or is not a historical fact. And we may fairly confine ourselves to the question whether our own species can be said to have progressed, not during the half million years or more which we sometimes call pre-history, but in the few thousand years since our ancestors began to use rough tools and to domesticate the wheat-plant. It will be equally within our scope to ask what are the prospects of our race in the future.

Ours is not the only species which has attained civilisation. It would be absurd to deny the word to the social insects—ants, bees, wasps, and termites. These creatures have elaborated a very complicated organisation, and have lived for long ages in a stable equilibrium. The beehive is a suffragette millennium, a gynaecocracy of maiden aunts. Specialisation in these societies goes far beyond anything that we have achieved by division of labour. It depends on the position of the queen-bee's body whether she lays a fertilised or an unfertilised egg. The fertilised eggs have been in contact with the store of sperms deposited in her body during her single nuptial flight, which is immedi-

47

ately fatal to her husband. The fertilised egg becomes a queen or a sexless worker; the unfertilised becomes a drone, who therefore has no father.

Ants can talk to each other, but they use chiefly an 'antennary language'. They can be excited and depressed, pleased and angry. Some of them keep slaves, and the termites keep pets. Some ants store their food, and build cities, with houses connected by underground passages, extending, according to Forel, to fifty or a hundred square yards. They are said to use the stars to help them to find their way—which is a little difficult to believe. These are only examples of what we can only call a very elaborate civilisation, absolutely ruthless in its disregard for the comfort of the individual, but ingenious and effective to the last degree.

The orthodox view seems to be that at an early stage in the evolutionary process a choice (so to speak) is presented to different species, whether they will proceed by instinct or intelligence. Such is the opinion of Bergson, Sir Arthur Thomson, and, I suppose, most scientific authorities. Instinct works admirably so long as conditions remain the same; but it has no power of adaptation to a changing environment. It is conceded that some of the lower animals have a slight power of intelligent response to a new challenge, but their lives on the whole are regulated wholly by instinct.

I find it difficult to believe that anything but intelligence, and intelligence of a high order, taught the wasp exactly where to sting its victims in order to paralyse without killing them, taught the bees the best geometrical form for their cells, and the spider how to make its web. Is it necessary to postulate this generic difference between instinct and intelligence? Let us suppose that the social insects, before man appeared on the scene, went through a long period of 'progress', gradually discovering, by experiment, trial and error, all that they needed for a perfectly ordered social life. At last the problem was solved; a stable equilibrium was reached. From that time onward the restless intelligence was a positive drawback and danger to stability. So nature withdrew that faculty, leaving only unconscious racial memory. The beehive, the ant-hill and the termitary need robots, automata, not thinking citizens. They are in purgatory, and it is better that they should not know it. Intelligence, in fact, is a rare device of nature to enable a species to adapt itself to a new environment. When the conditions are stable, a species is better without it.[1]

If this view, which I suppose is scientifically heretical, is true, may we expect something of the same kind to happen to our own species? Are there not already many signs of the depersonalising of man, the forcible suppression of individuality, the banishment and disparagement of intelligence? Is it not the avowed object of the totalitarian State to turn its citizens into automata? Let us suppose that in the art of war this type of State establishes its superiority over the democracies, so that they are obliged either to succumb or to adopt the methods of their conquerors. In each generation the opposi-

[1] I can find scientific support for this view. 'Instinct began in a reasoned act. This act, through being continually repeated, tended to lose the reasoning element and to become more and more unconscious. As this process continued through generations, the mental machinery through which it worked got more indelibly engraven in the mind. And in the end it became automatic—in other words it became instinctive.' Hingston, *Problems of Instinct and Intelligence*, p. 268.

tion would become more feeble, till it found expression only in a few scattered individuals who would be easily 'liquidated'. Under a perfect State-socialism there would be no more individuals, but only cogs in the machine. Science might possibly show how to 'condition' children for their future places in society, as in Aldous Huxley's *Brave New World*. There would then be an end of progress, unless some other more enterprising species is secretly preparing to carry on the torch in our place.

This would mean a biological change, and the resistance to it would be persistent and probably successful. But it is wholesome to envisage such a possibility, which already seems less chimerical than it did fifty years ago.

Let us pass to another line of enquiry, and interrogate human history. No one supposes that progress has been uninterrupted. Even those who believe that the course of humanity has been steadily upward have compared it to a spiral, not to a straight line. Others have thought that the 'vicious circle' gives a truer image. Tennyson rightly sees 'many a backward-streaming curve'. There has in

fact been one disastrous retrogression within
the historical period—the six hundred years
or so which followed the fall of the Roman
empire in the West. We must never confuse
the Dark Ages with the Middle Ages. In the
eleventh century the tide was beginning to
turn, and the centuries which followed were
an extremely interesting period, which made
permanently valuable contributions to civilisation. We should not have lost much if the
centuries between 500 and 1100 had been
blotted out. It follows that all who are concerned with the philosophy of history and
the prospects of humanity must try to find
an answer to a very difficult question—why
the Graeco-Roman civilisation, which in the
second century was still so flourishing,
collapsed and gave way to a long period of
barbarism. Such things, it seems, may happen. They have happened once and may
happen again. There is no cosmic law to
prevent the death of a culture.

The problem has been discussed many
times, and many causes, most of them only
symptoms, have been adduced. The question
really is whether all these causes put together
are sufficient to account for the fall of an

empire so widely extended, so rich and
powerful and civilised, to give place to barbarians whose institutions were on a much
lower plane.

What is the normal process of the dissolution of a great military empire? We
may mention two causes—the difficulty of
controlling distant provinces from one centre, and the rebellion of conquered nations.
It is usual for the central government to
delegate its power to satraps, pashas, or vice-
roys, who after a time try to make themselves independent. This process broke up
the empires of Alexander, the Saracens, the
Turks, and the Great Mogul. This danger
threatened the Roman empire, but it was
surmounted. There were numerous civil
wars and successful usurpations; but it was
only in the third century that attempts to set
up independent kingdoms were for a short
time successful. The disorders of this period
inflicted irreparable injuries on the empire;
but the Sultanate of Diocletian and his successors triumphed over these fissiparous ten-
dencies, and only the inevitable division of
East and West established itself, until the
Western empire was broken up.

Nor was it destroyed by internal revolt. As a rule the provinces, once conquered, remained conquered, and even became proud of belonging to the empire. There were fierce revolts during the process of conquest in Gaul and Britain. But the Jews were the only nation which rose in fury against their conquerors, and Palestinian nationalism was wiped out. The provinces were allowed to govern themselves so long as they kept quiet; there was very little vexatious interference with their religion, language, and customs. Under the republic they were pillaged ruthlessly, but under the empire the administration was fairly good.

Nor had the Roman armies much difficulty in repelling invaders, until the battle of Adrianople in 378, when the heavily armed Gothic cavalry broke the legions and began a long period of supremacy for mounted troops.

Barbarian invasions were nothing new. Not to go back to the battle of the Allia, there was a very formidable invasion at the end of the second century B.C. These inroads were for plunder or settlement; there was no hatred of Rome. Germans were already numerous in the Roman army in the first century; they were pensioned with lands in the empire held on military tenure. Before long the confession that in the army the effective force was no longer Italian became undeniable. Barbarians, properly drilled, were now better fighters and above all cheaper than Roman citizens. Many Germans rose to high commands, and regarded themselves as soldiers of the empire.

Remembering then that Julius Caesar gave the empire two centuries, not of unbroken peace, but of more stable conditions than have existed ever since in the Mediterranean basin, why was there not a great increase of population and of wealth? Why did not the Romans overflow into the adjoining lands?

Rostovtzeff speaks of the tyranny of the army as a proletarian revolt. This is, I think, a mistake; the army thought of no interests except its own. It favoured the elevation to the purple of able officers, but murdered them when there was a prospect of a new 'donative'.

I shall in this book protest against the modern fashion of rewriting all history in

terms of economics. But in this instance
economic retrogression is really the main
key to the mystery. The dishonesty of the
Roman mint was impairing and finally ruin-
ing credit. The *aureus*, which in the time of
Caesar was worth 27 francs, in the time of
Septimius Severus contained 50 to 60 per
cent. of base metal. In Egypt the *artaba* of
corn, which had been worth seven or eight
drachmas in the second century, cost 120,000
drachmas at the end of the third. This is
inflation on the German scale. The *antoni-
anus*, struck by Caracalla, soon became nothing more than a metal assignat. Diocletian
and Constantine re-established the currency,
but it was too late. Monetary economy was
already giving way to natural or domestic
economy. Why was this?

Capital was not applied, to any large extent, to industry. The great houses supplied
their own needs, as the estates of the Russian
nobles did till the revolution. The technique
of the crafts made hardly any advance,
partly because slave-labour discourages invention, and partly because there was no
scope for large-scale industry. The population of the empire was much smaller than

used to be supposed, and their wants were few. Rome probably never had more than half a million inhabitants. The area covered by most ancient towns is approximately known; they could not possibly have contained the large numbers of people named in the older books. The whole empire under Augustus may have numbered fifty millions. Only Egypt and North Africa were thickly populated. From the third century, most towns shrank into mere fortified redoubts.

The towns were not centres of industry. The wealth of the Roman governing class was almost entirely predatory. Their wealth came from abroad; bullion plundered from the eastern provinces, corn from Sicily, Sardinia, and Africa, rents from *latifundia*, shameless usury, and above all from slaves. With the dearth of slaves after the period of conquest was over, the value of land rapidly fell.

But why did the population fall off? There were destructive epidemics, but a healthy society soon makes up both these losses and those caused by war. For instance, the Great War cost ten million lives of men killed in action, and the world-wide epidemic of

57

influenza in 1918 killed from twelve to fifteen millions. But in 1928 there were more people in the world than in 1914, with probably quite as much wealth. But the Roman population did not recover. There is some truth in Seeley's opinion that the empire declined 'for want of men', with which Seeck couples 'die Ausrottung der Besten'. Depopulation and dysgenic selection; these are real causes.

Depopulation is a rather rare phenomenon, though the great increase of the white races since the industrial revolution was abnormal and in fact unique. The chief examples of depopulation in history have been in Greece, in Italy, in Spain after the sixteenth century, and in barbarous tribes whose country has been occupied by white men. Among these tribes new diseases, such as measles, have made great ravages; but the cause has been partly psychological—failure of the will to live. In New Zealand, where the native population at the time of the annexation was estimated at 100,000, the numbers fell to 40,000 at the end of the century. The Maoris believed themselves doomed. Since then they have recovered their high spirit, and now number 70,000. They are increasing faster than the whites. The Guanches of the Canary Islands and the Indians in the large West Indian islands are said to have committed race-suicide, and the Marquesas islanders are dying out.

The Greeks were prolific while colonies were available. But the mainland and the islands could not support a large population, and the soil became exhausted. Wars and frequent massacres thinned the male population, and infanticide was so common that it is a rare exception to read of more than one daughter in a family. In the graveyard at Gela there are 233 'potted' burials out of 570. Polybius mentions the reluctance of parents in the better class to have more than one or two children. There was, however, a large emigration to the east after Alexander's conquests, and Juvenal complains that Rome is a 'Greek city'. This emigration, like that from Spain after the discovery of America, partly accounts for the depopulation of Greece.

At Rome the decline began long before the end of the republic. In 164 B.C. there were 337,452 men capable of bearing arms, in 131 only 318,823. By the fourth century A.D. Bologna, Piacenza, Modena and many other north Italian towns were in ruins. What were the causes? A slave population never keeps up its numbers. In the West Indies between 1822 and 1832 the slaves registered diminished by 60,219, exclusive of manumissions. Malaria, perhaps a new disease in Europe, ravaged Campania, Latium, and parts of Greece. Deliberate restriction of the family is proved as regards the upper and middle classes. Many fled from the towns to escape the ruinous taxation. In one way or another, all the old republican families, except the obscure Anicii, disappeared.

But the main cause of depopulation in the Roman empire was the exceedingly high death-rate. Statistics are admittedly inadequate, but Macdonell, working on figures from the Corpus of Latin Inscriptions in the Berlin Academy, found that whereas in England the expectation of life at the age of fifteen is 45 years for males and 48 for females (it is now 51 and 54), at Rome it was 20 and 15 (*Biometrika*, vol. ix). The higher mortality for women is very remarkable. The figures for Spain are only a little better, for Africa decidedly better. These figures are chiefly for the free population; the slaves in *ergastula* probably died like flies. We do not know the birth-rates, but these figures are enough to account for a steady decrease. The rural population of Italy before the Punic Wars must have been much healthier.

Rome itself was an octopus, consuming much and producing nothing. It became a *colluvies gentium*, in which most of the population were on the dole. But most of the towns were unproductive, and when for fiscal reasons a regular caste system was introduced all hope and energy vanished. The only class which was not ruined was that of the large landowners, who lived on the produce of their farms (rents were now paid in kind), and gave shelter to a multitude of refugees from the towns. They soon began to keep armed bands, and defied the tax-collector. This was the beginning of the feudal system, which lasted in Europe for some fifteen hundred years.

The decline in literature, science and art from the second century onwards was as unmistakable as that of population and wealth, though here we must not forget the great jurists, the Christian apologists and theologians, and the Neoplatonic philosophers. The question may be raised whether in art and literature any further progress on the old lines was possible. Perfection once reached, only imitation and antiquarianism remained. We may perhaps venture to say that even the best Greek art was in danger of being conventional and monotonous.

The fact of exhaustion in almost every department of life is undeniable. Some of the causes have been mentioned, but the question has not been fully answered. I am disposed to give great importance to the psychological factor, the loss of hope and *taedium vitae*; but this again is a symptom to be accounted for. Under the late Roman Empire there was a change in the standard of values. Civic patriotism was dead. No one any longer believed in the Olympian gods. Orientals could see no beauty in Greek art; they were themselves ashamed of their bodies. Mystery-cults and theosophical religions more and more occupied men's minds. The world in which they lived had ceased to be interesting.

The *populus Romanus* no longer existed.

Its fate was that of most beasts of prey, though imperial Rome was the noblest beast of its kind. The name of Rome was and still is a symbol to be venerated; but the Latin nation lost its character and finally its existence in conquering the Mediterranean world. First, 'conquered Greece conquered her rude conqueror'; next 'the Orontes flowed into the Tiber'; then, thinking of the Roman army which was no longer Roman, Rutilius could say, 'it was a captive before it was conquered'; and at last the doom of the eternal city came in sight. It was no longer Virgil's '*imperium sine fine dedi*'; the Christian Juvencus writes, '*immortale nihil mundi compage tenetur; non orbis, non regna hominum, non aurea Roma*'.

What lessons can we learn from this catastrophe in reference to our own times? The danger of depopulation has in my opinion been far too much emphasised. Race-suicide is, as we have seen, a possibility, but one of rare occurrence. It is ridiculous to deny that a country may be over-saturated with people, and when a nation can exist only by importing food in large quantities, it should be plain that if its foreign trade declines, its population must decline too, or subsist on a lower standard of living. This alternative is being forced upon us in England, and the masses, who have won for themselves a degree of comfort unknown before, will restrict their numbers rather than lose it. The upper and middle classes have long ago faced this necessity. For it must be recognised that a high standard of living may be a handicap to a nation which is obliged to compete for external trade with other peoples who are, as we put it, in a more backward condition. Emigration would be the best solution. But it is the pinch of want which drives men to emigrate; our people (I do not blame them much) prefer to live on 'social services' and the dole, that is, on the tax-payer. But it is most unlikely that our countrymen will commit race-suicide. The fall in our birth-rate touched bottom, at least for the time, five years ago.

As for the 'Ausrottung der Besten', dysgenic selection is an unfortunate fact, whether our class-conscious socialists like it or no. But its importance has been exaggerated, and it may not be a permanent one. The main danger is not the extinction of our old fami-

64

lies, however much we may regret the loss of a national tradition. For though the founder of a family, unless he was a merely acquisitive collector of land, stocks and shares, may have been an exceptional man and perhaps a good sire, his descendants after one or two generations have probably reverted to the average. History shows many instances—we may think of Marcus Aurelius, Cromwell, Goethe and Napoleon—in which the son of a great man has been mediocre or worse. But if the cream of the working class in each generation is skimmed off and promoted by State aid, through scholarships at the universities, to the sterile professional class, the intellectual level of the population must be, to that extent, lowered. It is an inadequate compensation that the average ability in the professional class will be raised when it is no longer staffed only from one section of the nation. However, the ambitious board-school-boy will soon learn that the golden age of the professions is gone for ever, and that he will very likely gain nothing by leaving his own class. When I was in America I heard of two scientific demonstrators who had thrown up their jobs in order to become bricklayers, the wages of a bricklayer being considerably larger than the stipend of a lecturer in natural science. The approaching fall of our public schools, which personally I regret, will promote the abolition of class distinctions. In the Scandinavian countries, where all boys are usually educated together at the State schools, the differential birth-rate has almost disappeared. As for the upper class in this country, they will probably be completely ruined by inflation and predatory taxation. Having nothing more to lose, they will be less influenced by prudential considerations than they have been in the past. Marriages which would not long ago have been considered derogatory or imprudent are already very common, though too often such marriages are purposely sterile.

Improvements in technology are reducing the number of hand-workers necessary to maintain our industries. This alone will make some decrease in our numbers inevitable, for no State can go on maintaining a huge army of voluntary or involuntary idlers. We must hope to see a resumption of emigration, failing which we are not likely to be allowed to keep our valuable and half-empty dominions. At present it looks as if we are going to throw away a unique opportunity of peopling a large slice of the habitable globe with our own flesh and blood.

War and revolution are the two things which may wreck our civilisation. A recurrence of great wars, like that of 1914-1918, especially if they were exacerbated by quasi-religious fanaticism, would be as fatal to human progress as the chaos of the third century was to the Roman empire. Revolutions might be even more destructive; but the failure of the Russian revolution to spread westward, and the miseries which it has caused, give ground for hope that the civil upheavals which began in France in 1789 are not likely to be a permanent feature of civilised societies, though grave disturbances may be predicted after the present war.

But before leaving the Roman empire there is one more point to be considered. If instead of enumerating the signs of decadence in wealth, population, and intellectual activity we turn our attention to the moral condition of Europe at that time, a much more favourable verdict must be pronounced.

It is important to realise that a decaying material civilisation may be contemporaneous with a real advance in the spiritual life. In this way there may be a slow preparation for a new flowering-time, a new era of culture. In the fifth century there were signs of a new cult of Rome, her crimes forgotten and her benefits remembered. The beautiful eulogy of Claudian—'*haec est in gremium victos quae sola recepit*', etc., is well known, and the brave line of Rutilius, '*ordo renascendi est crescere posse malis*' contains not only the word but the promise of a long-retarded 'renaissance'. The Christian Church was not, as has been sometimes said, the cause of the ruin of the empire; it provided the soil out of which a new culture could grow. Other-worldliness alone can transform and revivify a dying world, though the two worlds must not be too sharply separated.

The swinish and heartless luxury of the rich at Rome, which culminated in the reign of Nero, became unfashionable under his successors. The treatment of slaves was more considerate. Pliny the Younger says that he is stocking his farms with slaves who are expensive because they must be trustworthy (*frugi*). 'No one about here keeps chained gangs.' The exploitation of the provinces was checked by authority. As regards sexual morality, we find a new tone about prostitution in Musonius Rufus, Dion Chrysostom, and Epictetus. Homosexuality was condemned with increasing severity; Plotinus would not stay to hear a speech which justified the practice. The morals of the Christian Church in the second century seem to have been extraordinarily pure; and though the Pagan mysteries varied greatly and were sometimes disreputable, the more that we know about them the more certain it becomes that they had a strong influence for good on those who sought initiation into them. Asceticism was already prescribed by Pagans as well as by Christians. The process of initiation included painful rites, such as fasting and flagellation. In a villa outside Pompeii there is a wall-painting of the lady of the house being whipped as part of her initiation. Most of the genuine religion at this time (and it was a very religious age) was attached to these associations, from which the Christian Church borrowed much of its ceremonial and its methods of discipline. Both personal religion and private morality advanced during the period of social and political decline.

What are we to say of Western civilisation in our own day? Is morality progressing or declining? In matters of sex there has certainly been a falling back from the rigid conventions of the Victorian age. No doubt even then a great deal of licence was winked at, and the aristocracy, though compelled to accept the alliance of the middle class and to pay outward respect to their standards, still retained much of the freedom of the Regency. But the gulf between virtuous women and the 'Corinthians' was immense. There has probably never been a period when female virtue was so immaculate as in the reign of Victoria. Literature was not only pure but puritanical; very few modern novels would have been accepted by a nineteenth-century publisher. The relaxation of moral strictness began after the death of the old Queen, and the Great War, as usually happens, encouraged almost promiscuous licentiousness. On the other side it must be remembered that within the last twenty years commercialised vice has declined enormously.

70

Looking at the moral condition of the world generally, and using morality in the wider sense, I am reluctantly obliged to agree with Aldous Huxley that 'judged by the only acceptable criterion of progress it is manifestly in regression'. 'Instead of advancing towards the ideal goal, most of the peoples of the world are rapidly moving away from it.' The only acceptable criterion is the advance of disinterestedness, of detachment from selfish, materialistic and narrow interests, what Dr. Marett calls progress in charity. Real progress has never been continuous; advance has alternated with regression. The eighteenth and nineteenth centuries were periods of progress; the twentieth has ushered in a sharp change for the worse.

Let us consider first the recrudescence of cruelty. This, which until lately was the one absolutely unpardonable sin among us, finds no place in medieval casuistry among the deadly sins; but the lay morality of the last century revolted against it. It would be superfluous to enumerate the achievements of humanitarian legislation. Even pessimists were unable to deny that modernity was far

71

more humane than earlier periods. The Victorians would have been incredulous if they had been told that torture and religious persecution would soon be reintroduced in civilised countries.

But what do we see now? In Germany savage floggings and other forms of torture are part of the machinery of government. The secret police visit private houses and sometimes murder the inmates in cold blood. In Russia horrors have been perpetrated to which history shows no parallel. Several millions of human beings have been slaughtered or deliberately allowed to die of hunger. Whole classes have been systematically exterminated. In Spain, where the absurdly misnamed Loyalists fought under the hammer and sickle and received orders from Moscow, the victims of the terror numbered at the lowest computation two hundred thousand; the official estimate is three hundred thousand. Their only crimes were either that they belonged to the middle class, or that they were attached to the Catholic Church. Fourteen thousand or sixteen thousand bishops, priests, monks and nuns died for their faith. Nor were the Reds content with simple murder. It would be easy to draw up a long and terrible indictment, guaranteed by eye-witnesses, of the frightful cruelties committed by them wherever they were in power. But one example will suffice. An American eye-witness (Helen Nicolson, *Death in the Morning*), says that at Ronda, a town near Malaga, 'they methodically exterminated whole families in the most fiendish fashion. First they impaled the men alive on stakes, and as this is a slow death the tortured and dying victims were forced to watch the fate of their wives and daughters, who were first raped before their eyes, and then drenched with petrol and burnt alive.'

St. Paul speaks of men who 'not only do such things, but take pleasure in them that do them'. There was a time, not so very long ago, when Gladstone toured the country denouncing the Turks, who had massacred twelve thousand Bulgarians in the district of Philippopolis. No doubt he wished to discredit Disraeli's government. No doubt he was unfair in blaming it for not stopping the atrocities. No doubt it was absurd to represent the Christian subjects of the Porte as innocent lambs. Sir Wallis Budge told me a

73

hideous story of the treatment of Turkish women and girls by Armenians. Even in Greece I have seen a picture in an illustrated newspaper, called *Boulgarophagos* (the 'Bulgarian-eater'), showing a Greek soldier gnawing the face of a Bulgarian. But the indignation of the British people at the atrocities of the Bashi-Bazouks was deep and genuine. Our people then loathed cruelty: do they now?

The murder of the Russian royal family, the emperor and empress, their four pretty daughters and their invalid son, was received in this country with ominous calmness. The wholesale massacres which followed in no way deterred the whole Labour party from expressing warm sympathy with Lenin and his satellites. More recently the leader of that party in the House of Commons actually went to Spain to assure the Spanish communists of the complete sympathy of British Labour with their cause.[1] It is needless to say that a number of young intellectuals, intoxicated by communist propaganda, were enthusiastic 'on the side of the assassins'.

[1] Those who are still unconvinced should read Krivitzky's *I was Stalin's Agent* (Hamish Hamilton).

74

Fanaticism is the most cruel temper in the world. But the grandparents of the working men who support Major Attlee would have recoiled in horror from professing friendship with these devils. I am quite unable to account for what looks like a real reversion to the worst kind of savagery openly approved by men who themselves have perhaps never killed anything larger than a wasp.

Together with this shocking evil we note a decline in men's regard for truth. 'At no period', says Huxley, 'has organised lying been practised so shamelessly, or so efficiently or on so large a scale as by the dictators of the present century. Most of this organised lying takes the form of propaganda, inculcating hatred and vanity and preparing men's minds for war. The principal aim of the liars is the eradication of charitable feelings and behaviour.'

War, with the nationalism which ends in war, is the villain of the piece. A tradition of violence is formed, and a perverted scale of values. The nation is personified, and ordinary decent behaviour is not expected of the national person, though it may be demanded in other national persons, his rivals. In preparing for and waging war, even democracies are fascised. Under dictatorships men are depersonalised and divested of moral responsibility. The conscience of the citizens, which ought to keep in check the unscrupulous actions of irresponsible power, is gagged and stifled.

A historian of morals ought to consider in what ways the institutions of a country at succeeding periods affect for good and evil the prevailing standards of conduct. For instance, in the last century the middle class was in the saddle. What is the type of character which is likely to be highly esteemed in such a society? The qualities which will be most honoured will be those of the respectable man. The respectable man is clean-living, temperate, industrious, thrifty, and law-abiding. In politics he will favour peace and retrenchment; it is the middle class, not the aristocracy or the wage-earners, which is strongly opposed to militarism. The faults into which this type is prone to fall are a too great preoccupation with money, and an over-emphasis on the importance of comfort. We may remember a once-popular hymn—

'Tis religion that can give
Sweetest pleasures while we live;
'Tis religion must supply
Solid comforts when we die.

The notion that beatified spirits live in a state of solid comfort is as characteristic of middle class mentality as the Mohammedan paradise is of the tastes of the Oriental.

But though the middle class set the tone of Victorian civilisation, it comprised neither the whole nor the majority of the nation. The aristocracy, deprived of its privileges but not yet of its prestige, had the usual faults of a favoured class, but was never a functionless body, like the old noblesse in France. It was probably the best aristocracy that the world has seen. The masses, who were debarred from profiting by the culture of their generation, were only gradually rising from the brutalised condition of the Georgian age. Drunkenness was often spoken of as the national vice, though beer-drinking was not so destructive as gin had been under the first two Georges.

The changes now in progress have come insidiously, and their importance is hardly yet realised. In another chapter I shall call

77

attention to the decrease in the importance of money, and to the consequent diminution of acquisitiveness. There has also been a change in ideas about the sacredness of private property, and the limits of justifiable State interference with it. Even in America, the most Conservative of civilised States, taxation has been introduced which forty years ago would have been vetoed as unconstitutional by the Supreme Court. The partial or total repudiation of public obligations by means of inflation, which in the last century was considered a disgraceful proceeding worthy only of disreputable Dago republics, has been accepted by all the belligerents in the Great War except Britain and America, and we, after being robbed by our debtors, have defaulted to the United States. We shall almost certainly follow our neighbours into bankruptcy before the end of this war, and we no longer feel that we shall be utterly disgraced by doing so. 'The word of an Englishman' is no longer what it was when the middle class, jealous above all else of its commercial integrity, was in power. Another side of this change is that pauperism is no longer felt as a stigma.

In many ways the improvement in the material condition of the working class has had good results. Drunkenness is no longer common, and crimes of violence are comparatively very rare in this country. The British workman is not a proletarian; he is what is called on the Continent a *petit bourgeois*. The worst national vice now is betting among the working class and gambling among a section of the rich. It is possible that the monotony of factory labour is partly responsible for this morbid craving for excitement. Gambling among the aristocracy has always been common, though it was severely reprobated by the middle class.

I agree with Professor Toynbee, who in the fourth volume of his *Study of History* says that the abandonment of our traditional artistic technique is manifestly the consequence of some kind of spiritual breakdown. 'We have wilfully cast out of our souls the great masters who have been the familiar spirits of our forefathers; and while we have been wrapt in self-complacent admiration of the spiritual vacuum which we have discovered how to make, a tropical African spirit of music and dancing and statuary has made an unholy alliance with a pseudo-Byzantine spirit of painting and bas-relief, and has entered in to dwell in a house that it has found empty, swept and garnished.'

The alleged decay of religion must be dealt with very briefly in this chapter. The clergy naturally consider what is happening too much from the professional standpoint. They see their congregations falling off, and the parochial system breaking up. The Free Churches are in the same predicament; and if the Church of Rome is not suffering to an equal extent, this is easily explained. An authoritarian Church is better protected against the criticism of science and scholarship than bodies which allow the right of private judgment. The discredit which has fallen on nineteenth century ideals has tended to increase the prestige of an institution which has never believed in them. There is also a tendency to revert to the Catholic *philosophia perennis* in place of the various modernist systems which are found to be increasingly unsatisfying. The curious fashion which has led a dozen men and women of letters in England to become Roman Catholics may or may not be an important symptom. The reasons for their action are not always very apparent; but it is at least plain that educated men no longer feel ashamed of professing their allegiance to the most uncompromising form of Christianity.

In this chapter we can consider the subject only from the point of view of human progress. That the Christian revelation was a permanent enrichment of human life will hardly be disputed. But the actual religion of a people can never be very far in advance of the intellectual and moral standard of the stage of civilisation which they have reached. From the time when the Church conquered the Roman Empire in the fourth century, and indeed from a rather earlier date, Christian ideas began to modify secular civilisation, and conversely, pagan tradition affected the Church. In modern times a great part of Christian ethics has become an integral part of social life in Europe and wherever the white man has settled. If we compare western civilisation with the independent non-Christian cultures of India, China, and Japan, we find in the West greater strictness in sexual conduct, especially in the strong condemnation of homosexuality; we find that infanticide is almost as unthinkable as cannibalism; and that sympathy and readiness to help those who are in trouble are more generally practised than in the civilisations of Asia.

Has there been a serious decline in these fundamentals of Christian ethics? In our own country the Christian standard is generally accepted even by moralists who do not call themselves Christians, except in matters of sex; in this field, as I have said, more licence is claimed than would have been tolerated (in theory) in the last century. The view is often held that traditional Christian morality was stereotyped at a period when, for reasons independent of Christianity, the ascetic ideal, especially in this direction, was held in excessive honour. Christ Himself, it is said truly, was more tolerant of disreputable faults and more severe towards respectable faults than the middle-class Victorian. Recent psychology, which has emphasised the frequency of neuroses caused by repression of our natural instincts, encourages critics of traditional morality to say what many of them have long thought. One of the most important changes of public opinion in our time is the removal of the stigma upon birth-control. This practice, which fifty years ago was held to be an improper subject of conversation, is now almost universally condoned, except by the Roman Church, which in some parts still tries to stop it, while in others confessing priests are not ordered to ask questions. The resistance to the practice now proceeds from other than religious or moral objections. The militaristic States of the Continent are afraid that the supply of cannon-fodder may run short; and among ourselves there is a scare about depopulation which is shared even by some experts in demography.

Whether the next hundred years will be a period of progress or decline depends mainly on whether the nations will have had enough of war. Some think that this second stroke will be fatal to the patient, and they may be right. But the recuperative power of a vigorous civilisation is very great, and if not only peace but confidence is restored, so that the race in armaments may be stopped, I do not despair, though I cannot be very hopeful.

The changes in social organisation which are commonly expected will make the twen-

tieth century unlike the nineteenth. Bureau-
cratic government discourages progress by
paralysing private initiative and diminishing
the motives for bold experiment. Intra-
group competition, which it is hoped to dis-
courage, is at first very successful in stimu-
lating material progress. It is the mother of
invention, though it may end in exhausting
those who are subject to it.

There are still some who think that our
advance in material comfort is likely to continue. I do not think so myself, nor am I
convinced that it is desirable. I think we
shall be driven to simplify our lives and re-
duce our wants. There is still too much de-
ference to convention and fashion. The eman-
cipation of women, who are the chief up-
holders of convention, would be a gain here,
if they were emancipated from each other.
In the upper and upper middle class they
have perforce shed some of their prejudices.

There is so much question-begging about
the word progress that it might be wise not
to use it, especially when as a corollary of the
theory of progress anyone who resists the
current of affairs is called a reactionary. We
who have lived to see violent changes would

do well to eschew the talk of reaction altogether; it leads to absurdities. Are we to say
that the Christian Fathers and the French
encyclopaedists belonged to the same type,
the progressive, and that the Roman Stoics
and the Prussian Nazis belong to the same
type, the reactionary? Von Eicken sees in
history repeated examples of the development of one state of things into its opposite.
Greek philosophy, beginning as natural
science, ended in mysticism. Roman im-
perialism destroyed the nationalism which
was its impulse. The Church subjugated the
world which it had renounced; monachism
passed into theocracy. Revolutions, which
begin with the cry that the poor have nothing to lose but their chains, end in iron
tyranny and universal serfdom. Every institution ends in strangling the ideas which
gave it birth.

The only escape from this cyclic rhythm
is to set our affections on the absolute un-
changing values in which the nature and
will of God are revealed to us. No imagined
temporal felicity can satisfy us, since that
also must change and pass. But nothing that
truly *is* can ever perish; it belongs to the

eternal order. 'The heavens shall vanish away like smoke, and the earth shall wax old like a garment; and they that dwell therein shall die in like manner; but My salvation shall be for ever, and My righteousness shall not be abolished.'

II
DEMOCRACY

II

DEMOCRACY

The apotheosis of Democracy began rather more than a hundred years ago, but in the early years of the last century it was still indignantly denied that the government of the United Kingdom was democratic. Even when the effigy had been placed on its pedestal there were always a few who refused to fall down and worship. 'Que ferai-je de ce dieu-là?' exclaimed Quinet. 'O le curieux fétiche! Je l'ai vu de trop près.' Within the last twenty years it has become possible to criticise without penalty, and over much more than half of Europe the venerated idol has been thrown down, broken, and insulted.

In Conservative America it is still worshipped, but there Democracy is not the name of a form of government which is accepted as a phase through which the nations have to pass; it is a mysterious revelation of divine power and beneficence. On the last occasion when I visited the United States I culled from a medical journal the following exulting words: 'Uric acid is tottering on its throne. Democracy is advancing in medical theory as well as in political practice.' A Boston professor exclaimed: 'You cannot separate God and Democracy. For if we believe in God we believe in God's purposes, God's ideal, and that is believing in God.' The suppressed minor premiss, that Democracy is God's ideal, was too obvious to need stating.

Even in England the grinning fetish still stands erect, though a good deal damaged by the missiles thrown at it. As an example of the naïveté with which its worshippers still bring their offerings, I may take the volume on Democracy in the Home University Library, by Mr. Delisle Burns. The author shows a little bad temper when he declares that 'certain demagogues of the "upper classes" (in inverted commas of course) say that Democracy is bad because it does not permit *them* to rule.' The aristocratic demagogues seem to be Mr. Bernard Shaw and myself. I have never wished to soil my fingers with democratic politics, still less to be a dictator; but as both Mr. Shaw and I might have kept the country out of two disastrous

90

wars, Britain might have done worse than intrust its destinies 'even to a dean or a playwright'. It is rather worse than ill-temper when we are told that 'the ancient rhetoric of dying for one's country covers the real purpose of warriors in killing for one's country.'

I will allow Mr. Burns to expound his pathetic faith a little further. 'Any common man may discover what is good by the use of his own capacities.' 'The moral authority of a democratic government is based upon the fact that the will of the people is right.' The ballot box, it seems, is a Urim and Thummim for ascertaining the divine will.

'The principles of Democracy are merely the principles of science applied to public policy.' The principles of science! Democracy, as Sir Henry Maine says, would have prevented the reform of the calendar, forbidden the power-loom and spinning-jenny, and restored the Stuarts.

'The League system can operate only if a sufficient number of the States which support it are democratic.' Why? Because 'the advocacy of peace occurs under Democracy and not elsewhere'. This was not the opinion

91

of Lord Salisbury, who wrote: 'Moderation, especially in matters of territory, has never been a characteristic of Democracy. Whenever it has had free play, in the ancient world or in the modern, a thirst for empire, a readiness for aggressive war, has always marked it.' Mirabeau thought the same: 'Free peoples are more eager for war, and Democracies more the slaves of their passions, than the most absolute autocracies.' 'A Democracy', says Irving Babbitt, 'is likely to be idealistic in its feelings about itself, but imperialistic in its practice.' 'We Americans', he adds, 'have shown ourselves a consistently expansive, in other words a consistently imperialistic people.' This cannot be denied. They have annexed Texas, California, Porto Rico and the Philippines by force, Florida by treaty, and have bought New Mexico, Alaska, and Louisiana.

'The most powerful influence tending towards Democracy was the Trade Unions, for the advancement of *their own* interests: this is real Democracy.' Comment is needless.

'The increase of the franchise is contemporary with the invention of the telegraph, the telephone, and the radio.' What have these to do with Democracy, any more than the American whoop over the defeat of 'uric acid'?

'Democracy is the discovery of new truth.' A fitting conclusion to the volume.

This example has been chosen because the author is a publicist of repute. It illustrates the tendency to treat Democracy as something sacred and sublime, and to ascribe to it many achievements, some of them of very problematical value, which have nothing to do with it. We have had similar books by apologists for Christianity, in which every advance in civilisation is uncritically attributed to the Church, or to the spirit of Christianity working upon institutions. The time has now come when Democracy must justify itself by an impartial estimate of the benefits which it has actually conferred on nations which have adopted it. These benefits are certainly not unmixed. We may conclude that though it worked well on the whole in the last century, its drawbacks are now becoming apparent. It will then be easier to understand why it has been deliberately rejected by one powerful nation after another.

We may consider a government as democratic when all adult citizens, or at any rate all adult male citizens, have votes, and when the personnel of the government and the broad lines of its policy are determined by the votes of the majority. Strictly, the voters should govern directly; but as this is only possible in a small City State, the principle of representation must be admitted as democratic. If instead of representation we have delegates who have no freedom to vote except at the dictation of the electors, the government is certainly democratic; but debate is reduced to a farce, and in practice purely sectional aims are attained by rigid discipline. At present the speeches in the House of Commons, which seldom turn any votes, are unreal and dull. It has become a question whether Ministers of State ought to be members of the House, since they have to waste almost every day several hours which might be far more usefully employed. Representation in the true sense is a partial abdication of popular sovereignty, but it may be made voluntarily, in the belief that men chosen by the electors for their merit ought to have some freedom to use their judgment. Now that members of parliament are paid, this freedom hardly exists for the majority of the House.

Defenders of Democracy do not, if they are wise, advocate it as simply a form of government. It is often considered as a form of State and as a form of Society. As a form of State it implies only that the voters, under universal suffrage, are the ultimate court of appeal, or the body who appoint magistrates, conferring upon them, perhaps, extensive freedom in the exercise of their duties. But this definition would include a plebiscite, which has often been used in the service not of Democracy but of despotism.

Democracy as a form of Society rests on the idea of social equality. This need not mean economic equality, but it implies equality of consideration, equality before the law. This kind of equality does not depend on democratic institutions, but it is more likely to be found under popular government than under any other form; and therefore some who have no confidence in the political wisdom of the herd may favour Democracy as the best protector of that equality of consideration which is perhaps better called fraternity.

The real advantages of Democracy as a method of government may be summed up as follows.

It diffuses a sense of responsibility over the whole population. Under a despotism or an oligarchy the mass of the citizens do not think that the government of the country is their business. So long as their social customs and their religion are not interfered with, they will usually acquiesce in being governed and taxed without their consent, and many abuses may flourish which an enlightened public opinion would have removed.

Under a Democracy the people are educated, in the sense that they acquire a degree of political wisdom which is rarely found except in connexion with popular government. Revolutions are rare in this type of State because the government learns, almost by instinct, when compromise is necessary, and when the time has come to act.

Democracy has also blurred class distinctions, a change which even Conservatives welcome. Books like the once famous novel *John Halifax, Gentleman*, on which Amiel makes interesting comments, illustrate a phase of English social life which has almost

passed away. There was then a line of de-
marcation between those who had the right
to call themselves gentlefolk and those who
had not; this line in England, unlike most
continental countries, ran through the centre
of the middle class. Only a limited number
of professions were open to the son of a
gentleman without losing caste. These artificial distinctions were almost wholly bad.
They corrupted the idea of a gentleman, by
encouraging the notion that a different standard of manners and even of morals was
appropriate in dealing with equals and with
inferiors. It was not uncommon, when I was
young, to meet aristocrats whose manners
to those whom they considered their inferiors would not make them popular in our
day. The distinction between debts of honour
and other debts was used to cover downright
dishonesty. This, I regret to say, still sur-
vives, especially among fashionable women
who defraud their milliners. Under feudalism the grand seigneur made free with the
daughters of his tenants, and there were
examples of this in the Scottish Highlands
till within living memory.

Democracy is a fair weather political

creed. It works moderately well when a
nation is fundamentally united, and un
willing to carry quarrels to extremities. Bu
any powerful organisation within the State
which will stick at nothing can make demo
cratic government almost impossible. It can
not deal with anti-social conspiracies. Ir
practice, when a country is either engaged ir
a serious war or is in danger of revolution
democratic institutions are suspended, and
the liberties of the subject are drastically
curtailed.

In foreign policy Democracies are vacillat
ing and ineffective. This evil is mitigated ir
England by a very competent permanen
civil service; but even these officials canno
secure any continuity in government policy
still less carry through those far-sighted
Machiavellian designs which foreigners some
times attribute, most absurdly, to our na
tion. I remember how, on my first visit to
the United States, in 1906, I was lunching a
the White House with Theodore Roosevelt
A fellow-guest who was sitting near me
wished to talk business with our host. 'Mr
President,' he said, 'you will never ge
American capital invested in the Philippine

until we know whether we are going to stay there or not. We don't know where we are. There is no continuity in our foreign policy.' 'Continuity in foreign policy!' answered the President. 'There is no continuity in our foreign policy, and while we are a Democracy there never can be. Why, in a couple of years Mr. Bryan may be here. You seem to think I can issue ukases, like the Tsar; not that he can ukase them much now, poor man!' Then he turned to me. 'It is just the same with you; there is no continuity in your foreign policy.'

A good example of the weakness of foreign policy under a Democracy is furnished by the unfortunate interposition of our government in Abyssinia. Our government knew, and the people of this country did not know, that the Abyssinians could offer no effectual resistance to the Italians.

Accordingly Sir Samuel Hoare and M. Laval tried to get the best terms they could for the Negus by sacrificing part of his territory. The Frenchman no doubt was double-crossing us; to drive Italy into the arms of Germany would be a blunder when a European war seemed more than probable. But there was just a chance that Mussolini might accept the terms. It is possible that his original plan was to take part of Abyssinia, and 'peacefully penetrate' the remainder. But public opinion in England was roused to frenzy. A mortal blow was dealt to the League of Nations if one member of the League could attack and destroy another; and what remains of the value of treaties if a great nation can dishonour her signature with impunity? This last argument, which means so much to us, is simply unintelligible to a Fascist, for whom reasons of State override all considerations of honour and morality. The Italians were furious, and were prepared to fight if we applied effective 'sanctions' against them. We drew back, and suffered a grave diplomatic rebuff, besides doing nothing but harm to our protégés.

There have been even more recent and more disastrous interferences of ill-instructed public opinion in foreign affairs. I have some reason to believe that neither the Prime Minister nor the Foreign Minister was in favour of the overtures to Russia which ended in a most humiliating fiasco. The Labour Party (and we have a *National*

Government!) had persuaded itself that
Nazism is a 'dictatorship of the Right', and
therefore hateful to all good Socialists,
while Russia is not only pacific and unag-
gressive but in some incomprehensible way
democratic, and therefore their friend. The
facts of course are far otherwise. Russia and
Germany are governed in much the same
way, and become more like each other every
year. Both are State-Socialisms, or—which
is much the same thing—State-Capitalisms.
Stalin has never concealed his utter contempt for Democracy; he was not likely to
help France and England against Germany.
He betrayed first the Allies and then Hitler,
because he wished to bring about this war,
which he hopes may end in revolution in all
the three belligerent countries. His treachery, which it seems was a surprise to our
politicians, knocked the bottom out of our
war-policy, but it was too late to draw back.
Our statesmen are well-meaning men, and
not really stupid—but the *arbitrium popu-
laris aurae* has led them to a line of action
which may be our undoing. The immediate
sufferers are the Poles and Czechs, with
whom the French, but not we, had made

pacts. Ignorant idealism may sometimes have worse consequences than cynical *Realpolitik*.

But the gravest doubts of the value of Democracy are in the field of economics. It is admitted by most people that industrialism, while it has unquestionably raised the standard of comfort in the population generally, has enabled a few persons to accumulate an unreasonable amount of wealth. Feudalism had accustomed the nation to acquiesce in the existence of a class of magnates who lived on a splendid and ostentatious scale. An oligarchic duke was a little king in his own county, and kings have always lived magnificently. 'The Duke of Omnium', says Anthony Trollope, 'had about the same income as Queen Victoria. He was quite content that she should be Queen and that he should be Duke of Omnium.' But there is no particular reason why a brewer or a tobacconist should have the means of living in this style. Not long ago a brewer and a tobacconist who happened to die in the same year left twenty-three million pounds between them. In America some fortunes have been far larger. Andrew Carnegie was bought out by Pierpont Morgan for four hundred million dollars, and the wealth of Henry Ford is believed to reach astronomical figures. If we accept the maxim of the Utilitarians that a good government should aim at the greatest happiness of the greatest number—a very useful principle, though it has been much criticised—there can be no doubt that happiness would be increased by redistributing these enormous incomes or devoting them to public purposes, as Lord Nuffield does with his profits from the manufacture of motor cars. A temperate economist has suggested that a clear income of five thousand pounds a year can give its possessor all the advantages and pleasures that a reasonable man can want.

These arguments, generally expressed with less moderation, are part of the stock in trade of Socialists. Many who are not Socialists are inclined to think that graduated taxation may remove or greatly diminish these inequalities without subverting the economic system of industrialism, under which the aggregate wealth and population of the country have increased, as used to be said, by leaps and bounds. This is sometimes called Socialism, but is in reality a substitute for collectivism. The amount of money spent every year on social services is a kind of ransom paid by the rich. Any revolution which dried up this source of revenue would very seriously injure the masses who now profit by it. If we read manifestos and declarations of policy by the younger generation of Conservatives, we shall see that they regard this system of ransom as a necessity. They say nothing about economy and retrenchment. Even the Liberals, who if they were true to Gladstonian traditions might sweep the suburbs with a programme of reduced taxation, are afraid to do so. They are content to pick up the exiguous crumbs left to them by the Labour Party, and in consequence cut a very poor figure in our political life.

This readjustment of economic conditions is the chief work of Democracy, and those who think such a policy necessary or beneficial are content to have it so. But though it may have worked well in averting a social revolution, it is fundamentally unjust. The herd instinct at once accentuates and disguises pure selfishness. The old constitutional maxim, 'No taxation without representation', has been flagrantly violated. The country is now divided into two nations, not, as Disraeli says in his *Sybil*, the rich and the poor, but the taxpayers and the taxeaters. The taxpayers have been deprived of all effective representation; there is hardly a constituency in which they could return a member pledged to look after their interests. Every general election is an auction of the worldly goods of the taxpayer. 'The forms of corruption under a pure democracy', says Lecky, 'are far more detrimental to the prosperity of nations than those which existed in other days.' At present, or rather before 1939, when the rich were shorn still more closely, one-tenth of the population paid more than five-sixths of the taxes. An immense parasitic class is being created, which drains the wealth of the country and becomes itself deeply demoralised.

Whenever one class levies the taxes and another class pays them, we may expect to see not only an organised pillage of the minority but an orgy of wastefulness. The scandals of municipal government where the Socialists are in a majority on the councils are notorious. In the Great War it was estimated that more than two thousand millions of public money were wantonly squandered, since it was no one's business to stop the leakage. We are reminded of the remarks of the Emperor Tiberius in Tacitus: 'Industry will languish and sloth will increase, if no man has anything to hope or fear from his own conduct. All men will idly expect assistance from others, lazy themselves and a burden to us.' Emigration has ceased to be a remedy for unemployment; the dole now attracts many thousands of most undesirable immigrants from Ireland.

The only remedy is to withdraw the power of the purse from those who contribute little or nothing to the revenue. Plato would give this power to a propertyless and ascetic caste, nature's aristocrats. In this as in other ways he seems to look forward to a type of government like that of the medieval Church. We cannot expect to see anything of this sort tried. The plunder of minorities will go on until the loot is exhausted, unless the unwisdom of killing the goose that lays the golden eggs is realised. But the demoralisation of the recipients is a greater evil than the impoverishment of the victims. The self-

106

respect of the working class is being under-
mined.

In the last century, during the transition
from a mixed constitution to a pure Democracy, the possibility of an alternative to
popular government was never even thought
of. Politicians were treated with sincere respect. A large proportion of the space of a
daily paper was given to full reports of debates in Parliament. The 'silly season' was
that part of the year when Parliament was
not sitting, and when therefore the editors
of the popular Press had to fill their columns
with trivial matters unworthy of the intelligence of their readers. The silly season now
extends from January to December. In the
reign of Victoria the speakers in Parliament
were not only reported but read through
diligently by the heads of households. Now
these debates are seldom reported except in
brief summary, and very seldom read. No
other body has lost in prestige so much as the
House of Commons. Not only is it recognised that the debates are unreal, since the
members of the House are practically obliged to vote with their party, but the profession of politics is not regarded with re-

spect. This contempt for politics and politicians has gone further in other democratic countries than with us. In the United States, in some of the British Dominions, and in France it seems to be expected that a politician is likely to fall short of any high standard of integrity. In England the change in the personnel of the House of Commons is far from complete, many of the members belonging to the same social classes as those who sat in Queen Victoria's reign. This is probably the reason why there is still a fairly high tradition of character and ability in the House. But there would be a general agreement that the arts which bring a politician into notice are not those which indicate any fitness to govern the country. It is probably true that a smaller number of able and high-minded men care to mix in political life than were to be found fifty or a hundred years ago.[1]

[1] Anatole Beaulieu in 1885 expressed this judgment in trenchant language. 'The wider the circle from which politicians and State functionaries are recruited, the lower seems their intellectual level to have sunk. This deterioration in the personnel of government has been even more striking from the moral point of view. Politics has tended to become more corrupt, more debased; it soils the hands which take part in it, and the

There are therefore several deductions to be made from the enthusiasm which the word Democracy was expected to evoke in the days before the Great War. It is an experiment in the most difficult of all arts, that of governing human beings. And when we look at the experience of other nations, which have borrowed their institutions from us or from our former colony in North America, we may begin to doubt whether it is well suited to all European peoples. In any

men who get their living by it. Political battles have become too bitter and too vulgar not to have inspired aversion in the noblest and most upright natures by their violence and their intrigues. The élite of the nation in more than one country are showing a tendency to have nothing more to do with them. Politics is an industry in which, in order to prosper, a man requires less intelligence and knowledge than boldness and capacity for intrigue. It has already become in some States one of the most ignominious of careers. Parties are syndicates for exploitation, and its forms become ever more shameless.'

I was once sitting at table when Lord Grey of Fallodon was one of my fellow-guests. The question was raised whether politics was an honourable profession, and Lord Grey said, 'It is a filthy trade.' It must, however, be said in fairness that even under a mixed constitution, such as I prefer, shady things are often done. John Bright, according to Bishop Creighton, said, 'If the people knew what sort of men statesmen are, they would rise and hang the whole lot of them.' Cavour is reported to have said, 'What scoundrels we should be if we did for ourselves what we are doing for Italy!'

case, we have lately seen it deliberately rejected in one great nation after another.

'Universal suffrage has always heralded the end of popular government.' This dictum of the German publicist von Sybel was not supported by sufficient evidence, but it would be true to say that a complete Democracy is not and cannot be as democratic as its theory demands. Governments are never what they seem. An autocrat may be a demagogue, an elected president an autocrat. An attempt to make a government logical may bring it to ruin.

It is now more than ten years ago that Mr. Lloyd George raised a note of alarm. 'Democracy is in peril. The spreading reaction against Democracy is a serious movement which needs watching in all countries.' To attack Democracy used to be a kind of blasphemy; now it is openly derided on all sides, and especially on the Left Wing. It has become clear that, as Le Bon says, 'there is an evident and irreducible opposition between Democracy and Socialism.' The Russian Communists helped to destroy the Weimar republic by disclaiming any sympathy with the German Social Democrats.

Syndicalism, which is sharply contrasted with State Socialism by its hostility to the State, is openly contemptuous of Democracy. Pouget says, 'Syndicalism and Democracy are the two opposite poles which exclude each other.' 'If revolutionary Syndicalism triumphs, the parliamentary régime dear to the intellectuals will be done away with.' A syndicalist revolution, timed to coincide with a Sinn Fein rebellion, was being prepared in England for the autumn of 1914.

The Communists are equally out-spoken, and the Fascists agree with them. It is hardly worth while to quote the scornful language in which Marx, Engels, Lenin and Stalin denounce the utter incapacity of the stupid and swinish multitude to know what is good for them. No extreme Tory has ever used such expressions. Hitler and Mussolini have been quite explicit in repudiating Democracy as a political experiment which has been tried and has proved a conspicuous failure.

I shall not discuss Communism and the class-war, because I believe that they belong to the nineteenth century, and are now moribund. They are kept alive mainly by a group

111

of young intellectuals, who in our day play the same part as the self-styled philosophers in France before the Revolution. They intimidate the half-educated public, and spread a spirit of defeatism which undermines the defences of the social order. Their undiscriminating abuse of industrial civilisation is a wilful distortion of history, but it has been listened to by a large number who for one reason or another are discontented. The wonder is that in a country like England, where there is no restriction upon even the most violent attacks against existing institutions, these persistent efforts of propaganda have not had more success. The House of Commons at present contains one Communist and no Fascists. The large sums sent to England from Moscow have been thrown away.

But Fascism requires much more careful attention. The name has become a mere term of abuse, bandied about, especially in America, by various political factions as a missile to throw at each other. If Democracy was for a long time a blessed word, only to be pronounced reverentially, Fascism is a swear-word, to be uttered with a hiss and with flashing eyes. This is not the way to understand the most remarkable political movement of modern times. For Fascism, in one form or another, is the monster (if we will) spawned by the Great War, which though undertaken, as we asserted, to make the world safe for Democracy, has had the effect of convincing more than half the world that Democracy is not safe for itself.

I have just said that the new dictatorships are the result of the Great War. But the circumstances in the three countries, Russia, Italy, and Germany were very different. In Russia it was certain that the Tsarist régime could not survive an unsuccessful war, and no one who knew anything of Russian history could suppose that the fall of the monarchy would be followed by a democratic constitution. Nicholas II was the most incompetent Emperor Russia had ever had, and Lenin was a consummate strategist, a monster of cruelty and hatred, but not incapable of compromise when it was clearly necessary. His victory over the Whites and over rival republican parties was for some time doubtful, and was achieved only after civil war. A campaign of ruthless extermination followed. It is not necessary here to say more about Russia, where the first revolutionary leaders were convinced apocalyptic Marxists, who expected a world-revolution in a few years, even in England. The Russian Revolution, like the French, has devoured its children, and has passed into a new phase, nationalist, imperialist, and hierarchical. The transition of Communism into Fascism illustrates the intrinsic weakness of the former and the strength of the latter.

In Italy it is often said by the enemies of Fascism that the scare of Communism was factitious, the danger having been surmounted before Mussolini came into power. So far as I have been able to form an opinion, this is untrue. Revolutionary outrages were continuous till in July 1922, the Communists organised a general strike, which was to deprive the nation of its food supplies. In October the famous march upon Rome took place, and Mussolini, without violating the constitution, was made Prime Minister by the King of Italy.

The Italians, who had driven a hard bargain with the Allies as the price of entering the war, were dissatisfied with what they received at the peace. They were even more dissatisfied with the experience of parliamentary government. Mussolini, who had been a violent socialist agitator, was quick to perceive that Nationalism and not Socialism provided the strongest appeal that he could make. That this was so is a striking sign of the times. It may well be that this frenzied Nationalism, which has swept Italy and Germany off their feet, may ruin European civilisation in a succession of savage wars, resembling but far surpassing in atrocity the wars of religion in the century after the Reformation. Mussolini, a condottiere of genius comparable to Napoleon, though without his military ability, resolved to exploit Italian patriotism to the uttermost. He made no constitutional changes, and even patched up a concordat with the Vatican, which was as easy in Italy as it was difficult in Germany, because Italians who care for religion are almost all Catholics, and Catholicism is itself a totalitarian polity. A certain degree of terrorism was necessary, but it was very mild compared with what was judged necessary in other totalitarian States.

The success of the new régime in putting

a stop to disorder, regulating civil life in all its branches, and in increasing the military power and prestige of the nation, was so great that the large majority of Italians, so far as we can judge, are sincerely attached to the Duce and his methods. The loss of liberty is not very severely felt in a country where violence and anarchy had torn society in pieces a few years before. But the government could not dispense with vigorous propaganda. Every house is plastered with the word Duce, and flamboyant posters setting forth the glories and the destiny of the new Roman Empire are to be seen everywhere. The Abyssinian campaign was not popular, since the Italian soldiers knew that the Abyssinians mutilated their prisoners; but the acquisition of a large territory in Africa was felt to add dignity to the position of Italy, even though the new empire is not likely ever to pay its expenses or to offer a tempting home for Italian emigrants. Italy is now the jackal of Germany, with extravagant ambitions.

The growth of National Socialism in Germany is a more remarkable phenomenon. It is often said that the harshness of the terms imposed by the Allies is responsible for the downfall of the Liberal Republic. It is true that the conditions of peace at Versailles were severe. The mutilation of German territory was unwise, since this always rankles in the mind of the vanquished more than anything else. Our King George V showed more wisdom than his advisers when he said to a friend of mine not long after the beginning of the war, 'If we win this war, I hope we shall not annex a single square mile of territory.' The indemnity demanded from the vanquished was grotesquely beyond what they could possibly pay. The invasion of the Ruhr by France was an inexcusable act of aggression. The one-sided disarmament, contrary to the promises made at the time of the treaty, was another grievance. It was a great pity that our statesmen, who inherited a tradition of generosity and fairness after a victorious war, could not have a free hand in negotiating with Germany. After Waterloo we were able to settle matters without much interference from other Powers. A letter of Castlereagh to Liverpool is an admirable statement of what our policy at Versailles should have been. 'It is not our business', he

117

said, 'to collect trophies, but to bring back
the world to peaceful habits. The more I
reflect upon it, the more I deprecate scratch-
ing such a Power (as France). We may hold
her down and pare her nails so that many
years shall pass away before she can again
wound us. But this system of being pledged
to a continental war for objects that France
may one day reclaim from the particular
States that hold them, without pushing her
demands beyond what she would contend
was due to her own honour, is I am sure bad
British policy.' No words could better expose
the series of blunders which have entangled
us in our present miseries. We were unable
to veto the policy of France, which was to
hold Germany down by crushing exactions
and to encircle her with a ring of States
pledged to support France in any future war;
while at the same time we were able to prevent this policy from being carried out as
thoroughly as the French desired. It was in
any case a most dangerous scheme, and it
broke down completely. The allied States
which were to keep Germany in fetters have
either been conquered or have fallen away.
The Russian alliance has come to an end.

France was left with no friend in Europe except ourselves, and has now, to all appearance, betrayed and deserted us.

But it may be doubted whether the harshness of the terms was the chief cause of the revolt of the German people against the Weimar Republic. Strange as it may seem to us, who were astonished at the tremendous power of the German military machine, what wounded the Germans most was the fact that they had been beaten at all. They were obliged to persuade themselves that their victorious armies had been stabbed in the back by Communists and Jews. This legend is now the official doctrine.

It is possible that if the Allies had given a generous support to the Weimar Republic, Germany might have been content with a pacific and democratic government, in which the Social Democrats were the dominant party. But this is very doubtful. That government, though it was honest and fairly capable, did nothing to dispel the profound depression which hung over the country during almost the whole of this period. Nothing proves this more strongly than the fall in the birth-rate, which had been 36.0 in

1900, and was 14.7 in 1933. The latter figure was below what was necessary to keep the population stationary. In all the large towns demoralisation had gone so far that homosexuality, which the French call *le vice allemand*, was practised quite openly, catamites standing at the street corners and offering themselves. In 1929 the number of abortions in Berlin exceeded that of live births. The country seemed to be morally rotten, and nothing but a spiritual awakening could have saved it.

This awakening was due to Adolf Hitler, a young Austrian of humble parentage who had served with credit in the war, and after beginning his public career, like Mussolini, as a revolutionist, was seized with a fiery patriotic passion. He had no respect for the North Germans, whom he accused, oddly to our ideas, of stolid pacifism. But he was a born agitator, and had studied the technique of propaganda with great success.

His temperament is very different from that of the Italian Duce. Mussolini is an unbeliever, Hitler a fanatic. Mussolini is coolheaded, with an iron will; Hitler is neurotic and hardly sane. His hatred of the Jews is quite sincere, though revolting; it is a maniacal obsession. He is abnormal in other ways —ascetic in his habits and probably immune to the temptations of sex. Those who speculate on the chances of his downfall forget the most likely end of his reign, a complete mental breakdown. Power, as Lord Acton says, always corrupts; absolute power corrupts absolutely. Hitler is not likely to escape the doom which obscured even the hard and lucid intellect of Napoleon.

That such a man should captivate the rough and virile German character may seem amazing. But Nietzsche, with his uncanny penetration, knew better. 'The masses must have the impression that an invincible will-power is there. He must have all the qualities of the masses, for they will then be the less ashamed of them and he will be more popular. Let him be violent, envious, an exploiter, an intriguer, a flatterer, a crank. Let him be puffed up, and be everything according to circumstance.' The Germans, with all their practical qualities, are intensely sentimental and liable to be carried away by any myth which arouses their emotions.

The mentality of the dictators is hateful. Voigt says of them quite truly: 'Lenin and Hitler are quite unashamed in their constant advocacy of ruthlessness, of the bloodiest wars and upheavals. Throughout all Marxian and National Socialist literature there is not a trace of pity, magnanimity, forgiveness, or of any generous feeling, not one word of respect for honour or for righteousness—not one trace of toleration, not the slightest appreciation for a foe who might be brave, or even right in his own way.'

Fülöp-Miller characterises Bolshevism as a barbarous Jesuitism. The parallel is not an idle one. We cannot understand either Communism or Fascism until we recognise that both are a kind of religion, with the absoluteness and fanaticism which only religion can produce. The Duke of Alva and Torquemada would have been horrified by much that has been done by Communists and Nazis, but it is a question of degree. The old wars of religion and attempts to stamp out heresy show the same ruthlessness as these modern movements. The greater horror of the modern fury is due to the fact that it is nowhere restrained by the humane principles of real religion, which could not be entirely forgotten even by the most cruel of Catholic persecutors. The modern fanaticisms give to Caesar—we might almost say to the devil—the things that are God's. Especially characteristic of authoritarian rule is the violent suppression of all criticism of the government. Catholicism stigmatises doubt and independent thinking as a sin, totalitarianism as treason or sedition. 'Dangerous thoughts'—a delightful phrase invented by the Japanese—are themselves acts of rebellion. If one voice is allowed to be heard out of harmony with prescribed orthodoxy, the confidence of the faithful may be impaired. The minds of the people must be hermetically sealed against every disturbing influence. As Goebbels said in 1934, 'As we, the National Socialists, are convinced that we are right, we cannot tolerate any other in our neighbourhood who claims also to be right.'

And yet we must try to understand why a system which is obviously the negation of what we consider the fundamental rights of man, rights won by long struggles in all free countries, is enthusiastically supported not

123

only by the worst but by many of the best in at least two great countries. Fascism can point to great material achievements. In Italy, where the traveller used to expect to find not only unequalled charm of nature and art but dirt, thieving, begging, idleness and disorder, the trains now run punctually, the hotels are clean, the beggars and pickpockets have disappeared, the breeding grounds of the malaria mosquito have been drained, and fine motor roads are laid down all over the country.

In Germany this kind of cleaning up, except in the matter of sexual scandals, was not necessary. But Nazism has secured two results of first-rate importance—national unity and the restoration of confidence in dealings with foreign Powers. So grateful are millions of Germans for these benefits that they will not even admit that they have lost their freedom, though they dare not open their mouths without looking round to see whether anyone is listening. Lucan speaks of '*libertas, cuius servaveris umbram si quidquid iubeare velis*', and the Germans will not see that it is only the shadow, not the substance, of liberty which is so preserved.

It is a foolish or perhaps a wilful perversion of the truth to say that Nazism was the creation of big business. It is true that the danger of Communism was much emphasised at the time, and as over thirteen millions of voters had supported the Left, it is not surprising that alarm was felt. Lenin himself declared that Communism was stronger in Germany than in any other country except Russia. In reality the uncompromising Communists were never very numerous, and Moscow, as I have said, repudiated any connexion with German Social Democracy. But it was the 'little man', the *petit bourgeois*, who put Hitler in power. This class, despised by the Marxists, had borne arms, and had no mind to be 'liquidated'. In Germany as in the Western nations this class is the backbone of the community. The new system, though attacked from every side, advanced from strength to strength.

Italian Fascism is careful not to announce any programme, for a programme must invite discussion. Nazism would suppress not only intellectualism but the intellect. Drucker says that nothing made him understand

125

Nazism better than when he heard a speaker declare, amid wild and enthusiastic applause, that 'we do not want higher bread prices. We do not want lower bread prices. We do not want unchanged bread prices. We want National Socialist bread prices.' In Germany, which once held a position second to none in philosophy, science, learning and music, we have National Socialist history, science, art and scholarship, all alike contemptible. This is the temper of the soldier on campaign. 'Theirs not to reason why, Theirs not to make reply, Theirs but to do and die.' Do we wonder that any intelligent man should voluntarily degrade himself into the position of an automaton, a robot? This surprise would show an imperfect knowledge of human nature. Many of our soldiers in the Great War testified to the strange sense of relief at not having to use their minds at all, at having all decisions made for them. The cause of reform has always been impeded more by those who like to obey than by those who are accustomed to rule. The same desire for peace of mind at all costs is the cause of many conversions to Catholicism. After years of perplexity in the face of

126

contradictory theories and convictions, a man will cease to reason and will submit himself without reserve to dogmatic authority.

But it is not only logic and reason that the enthusiastic young Nazi has renounced, though he agrees with Voltaire that when the people begin to reason all is lost. It is the materialism and selfishness of Western civilisation. It is possible to prove that Nazism has not improved the condition of the majority of Germans, that hours of work are longer, wages no higher, taxation more severe, than before Hitler came into power. The Nazis will try to deny it, but in reality they do not care. When they are asked, 'Guns or butter?' they will shout, 'Guns', not because they want war, though they declare that death in battle is the noblest way to end one's life, but because the idea of making sacrifices of comfort for the sake of their country is one which fills them with enthusiasm. For the Germans the State is a god on whose altar they are proud to lay their offerings. Under Liberalism, the State exists only to serve the interests of the individual; under Nazism or Fascism the indivi-

127

dual exists only to serve the interests of the State.

The following extract from the article on Fascism in the *Enciclopedia Italiana,* by Mussolini himself, will illustrate the state of mind common to all convinced members of totalitarian States.

'To Fascism the world is not this material world as it appears on the surface, where Man is an individual separated from all others and left to himself, ruled by a law of nature causing him through his instincts to lead an egoistic and momentary life of pleasure. Man in Fascism is individual, nation and country all in one, and is therefore a party to the moral law which binds individuals and nations together into a tradition and a mission, and which in suppressing the instinct of a life enclosed in the short cycle of pleasure, bases a higher life, beyond the limits of space and time, on duty. Fascism is a religious conception of life, in which Man is seen in his inherent relation to a higher law. . . . The idea of Fascism is all for the State, and for the individual in so far as he coincides with the State. It is against Liberalism, which has reached the end of its historical

128

function. Liberalism denies the State in the interest of the individual. Fascism affirms the State as the true reality of the individual. For the Fascist, everything is in the State, and outside of the State nothing legal or spiritual can exist, still less be of value. The Fascist State is the unity and synthesis of all values.'

This ideal is not without its nobility. It recalls the lines of Ennius, in which he sums up the whole duty of man in the days when the Roman republic was storing up the force which made it the ruler of the Mediterranean world:

'*Commoda praeterea patriai prima putare,*
Deinde parentum, tertia iam postremaque
nostra.'

Our country first, our family second, ourselves last. But certain reflections suggest themselves. The deification of one's own State almost implies that no other States have a right to exist. If they have a right to exist, there are limits to the demands which our own State can make upon us. In the present condition of the world, there is a comity of civilised nations which are not absolutely separate from each other. The European nations, with their offshoots beyond the seas, are in a sense a unity. They share the same civilisation, the same traditions and customs, the same religion and philosophies. All alike derive their spiritual and intellectual heritage from Israel, Greece and Rome. Wars between these nations are in reality civil wars, no less than the constant struggles between the little cantons of ancient Greece, which ultimately destroyed the most highly endowed race which has ever existed on this earth, and the very similar wars between the brilliant Renaissance republics of Italy, the consequences of which were equally ruinous. Is modern Europe to perish in the same way? The doctrine of the God-State seems logically to lead to internecine warfare between States which do not allow to each other even the right to exist. It is not to be expected that States which demand unlimited sacrifices from their subjects, and which explicitly deny that there is any morality above the interests of their own State, will pay any respect to international law, to the sanctity of treaties, or to the usages which have hitherto mitigated the

ferocity of wars in Europe. We have seen
that no such obligations are recognised. But
this means that no nation is safe unless it is
stronger than any possible enemy. The fear
which is the cause of the ruinous competition
in armaments is too well justified when the
State is deified.

Except for defence or attack in war, what
justification is there for the claim of the
State to suppress all rights and liberties in its
subjects? These rights, the right to life,
liberty, and the enjoyment of property law-
fully come by and conscientiously used,
have for two thousand years been regarded
as natural rights, secured by the Law of
Nature which is older and more sacred than
any human enactments. A government
which transgresses these natural rights has
no moral claim on the obedience of its citizens, and is a standing danger to all its neighbours. It is a tyranny, and many medieval
casuists argued that tyrannicide is justifiable.

The gods, says Homer, take away half a
man's virtue when he becomes a slave. Under
a totalitarian State all are slaves, willing
slaves perhaps, but none the less slaves. This
is the conclusive condemnation not only of

131

Fascism but of all State Socialism and perhaps of all 'planned economy'. When every man's means of livelihood are at the mercy of State officials the citizens are handed over, bound hand and foot, to an omnipotent bureaucracy, who being exempt from criticism are not likely to remain honest or competent, and are certain to be arbitrary and tyrannical. A free people makes many mistakes, but it retains the power of correcting them. A dictatorship is not likely to give effect to reasonable public opinion, because it has taken every precaution to prevent public opinion from existing.

We are all members of many societies or organisations, each of which has a limited and indefeasible claim upon us. There is the family, our trade or profession, our place of education, our country, our Church, the whole comity of civilised nations, and humanity at large. Our highest duty in each of these spheres is summed up in our duty to God, that is to say, our homage to those absolute and eternal values in which the nature and will of the Deity are revealed to us. Some of these claims are narrower than the State, others still wider. What possible reason is there for singling out the State as the one all-embracing and absolute sovereign power? There is no special sacredness about the State. Is it not certain that not only other nations but other organisations will claim the same exemption from the moral law? Among these the Communist International has already asserted the same absoluteness. A civil war between a totalitarian State and an international ideology might be even more frightful than the kind of war to which we are unhappily becoming accustomed.

We are in fact in the presence of a false religion, the religion of Nationalism, which is far more dangerous than no religion at all. It bears on its banner the motto 'Duty and Discipline', and the call that it makes is answered with enthusiastic acceptance. Whether it will trample on all opposing forces as the French revolutionary armies did at the end of the eighteenth century remains to be seen, but the outlook is very menacing. We do not yet know the full extent of the risks which we ran when a vacillating government was goaded into a game of bluff with Germany in September, 1939. A

German victory would mean the end of Britain as a great Power; whether it would also mean the end of Democracy we cannot say. The United States will not change its form of government; but the remaining European democracies might conceivably be driven, under the stress of war, to accept the rule of the 'strong man', without intending to abandon popular government altogether. In Latin America dictatorship is the normal condition, and Spain is once more under military rule.

Abruptly to change one form of State into another would be difficult. For there is this essential difference, that in a totalitarian State every grade in the hierarchy is responsible to the grade *above* it, while under a Democracy the officials are theoretically responsible to those below them, to the electorate. In the former type the apex of the pyramid is the Emperor, Duce, or Führer. There is no reason why he should not be surrounded by an able body of advisers; but in practice it seems that there is a tendency for the dictator to remove all possible rivals, and to attach to his person only mediocrities and subservient characters. Stalin has almost made a solitude round him; it is difficult to say what would happen if he vanished from the scene. Mussolini and Hitler are believed to have made arrangements for the succession, and the régime would probably survive the first dictator for some years. But there is always the possibility that the dictator may become insane or incapable while still clinging to power. Hitler, as I have said, is certainly not normal, and may become a homicidal maniac or a pinchbeck Alexander. It would then be necessary to depose him, and this might be no easy matter.

If the views expressed in this chapter are correct, it seems that the peoples have only to choose between several evils, since all forms of government are bad. They are all bad, and bad in the same way, since they destroy the independence of the individual. 'Le moi d'un homme', says Victor Hugo, 'est plus vaste et plus profond encore que le moi d'un peuple.' The virtues of the State, says Proclus, here differing from his master Plato, are only images of the virtues in the individual soul. Individual morality has outstripped crowd morality by many centuries. The modern dictator seems to embody crowd morality at its worst. Tyranny is worse than socialistic bureaucracy, but may be shorter lived and less paralysing. Bureaucracies are strangled in red tape; the Jack-in-office may make himself extremely disagreeable, but he has very little initiative.

We cannot go back to the period between the first and second Reform Bills, when Lecky thought that this country was best governed. We shall probably make shift with Democracy for some time longer, and I am quite unable to guess what new experiment in government will follow it. I hope it will not be Fascism.

III
ECONOMISM

III

ECONOMISM

By Economism I mean the theory that economic questions, relating to the acquisition, production, and consumption of wealth, are the most important problems of social life, dwarfing all others into insignificance. History has been rewritten in accordance with this theory. We are told that the rulers of States, whether kings or senates, may have supposed that their policy was determined by the desire for military glory, for extensions of territory, or by religious enthusiasm; but if we look below the surface, we shall find that the wars of the past, like those of the present, were for markets or raw materials. When Rome destroyed, in the same year, Carthage and Corinth, it was because those cities were commercial rivals. In the early modern period Spain, France and England fought each other for the sake of overseas trade. Any other motive is hardly intelligible to our modern pundits.

Other motives have not always been unintelligible, and if the old histories were written from a different point of view, it is probable that this other point of view appeared to the contemporaries of the events described as the true one. The predominance of economics belongs to the nineteenth century; it created the mentality of the capitalist and of the communist, thereby setting its stamp on western civilisation for more than a hundred years. Economism is like a science of the stomach without knowledge of physiology or of other organs.

My contention in this chapter is that the unrest and dislocation of social life during this period was due not to defects in our institutions, but to a faulty standard of values, which generated bitter and unnecessary conflicts: I shall further maintain that this standard of values has been appreciably modified during the last twenty years, and that in consequence the old parties, with their shibboleths and war-cries, are out of date. The change has, I think, been salutary on the whole, but it has given rise to great evils, of which the chief is a revived glorification of war, with all its horrors and suicidal acti-

140

vities. The evil is part of a larger movement, a perverted romanticism calling itself realism, which has profoundly altered the outlook of the younger generation on the Continent.

Since Christianity is still the framework within which our standards of value are set, and since the teaching of the Churches has to a large extent coincided with the prevailing conceptions of social duties, it will be useful to consider briefly the attitude of the Christian Churches towards the questions which arise out of the economic life. It is only in our own day that the Christian tradition has been violently repudiated, and there are some signs, not clearly discernible at present, that a return to the Christian standard has already begun.

In early Christian literature there is no thought of what we call social, i.e. economic, questions. Christianity had its origin among a fairly prosperous peasantry, and its early converts belonged mainly to what we should call the lower middle class. Before the end of the first century a few even of the aristocracy had become Christians. It was a purely religious movement, individual and universal. It abolished all man-made distinctions

by ignoring them; it demonetised the world's
currency by treating wealth as of no account, or as a positive hindrance to a life of
detachment. The law of love was enough to
regulate our relations with our fellows—a
law which soon tended to be narrowed but
intensified by confining it to 'the brethren',
i.e. to fellow-churchmen. Its rule of life was
heroic rather than ascetic. It had no thought
of the State, but remained law-abiding and
aloofly loyal. All men are equal in God's
sight; therefore social distinctions, even slavery, do not matter, though worldly cares
should be reduced to a minimum.

The idea of a gradual amelioration of
human conditions through concerted effort
was entirely foreign to the early Christians,
as also to their Pagan contemporaries. But
while the latter were deeply concerned to
preserve the classical culture from being submerged in a welter of barbarism, the Christians were on the whole detached and indifferent, though the sack of Rome by Alaric
gave even St. Jerome a shock. It was only
after Constantine that ideas which sound
communistic are at all frequent in patristic
literature, and there was no attempt to

translate these into practice, except in the monasteries, and in purely voluntary charity.

During the Dark Ages which followed the disruption of the empire, the Eastern Church was subordinate to the State. There was no Renaissance and no Reformation in the East; religious revivals merely reinforced monasticism. In the West the Church assumed more and more the task of civilising a barbarous population. But the structure of society was now very simple, based on natural economy. Money played a very unimportant part in the life of the majority.

All through the history of the Church the problem of harmonising the Law of Nature, which knew nothing of laws, governments, and warfare, with the conditions under which fallen man was obliged to live, had exercised the Christian conscience. The tendency was to allow a double standard, the Sermon on the Mount for the religious who had renounced 'the world', and the life of an orderly citizen for the majority. In later Catholicism the distinction between 'nature' and 'supernature' partly took the place of the earlier teaching. In the sect-type of Christians, which of course existed before

143

the Reformation, the tendency was to reject all compromise.

At the Reformation, and especially at Geneva under John Calvin, the Church came for the first time into relations with the modern type of urban civilisation, based on a money economy. Lutheranism was still half Catholic and medieval; it was most at home in agrarian societies. It has often been said that Calvinism accepted capitalism, and encouraged the hard and unlovely type of society which resulted from the industrial revolution at the end of the eighteenth century. This is unjust to the Reformers, who were thoroughly alive to the dangers of the acquisitive life.

True Calvinism is ascetic, but its rigorous self-denial is practised within secular life. Its aim is to glorify God and produce the Holy Community. What is most characteristic of this branch of the Reformed Churches is its indifference to the results of its activities. Clough's lines:

'Go, say not in thy heart, And what then,
    were it accomplished,
  ere the wild impulse allayed, what were
    the use and the good?'

144

represent the mind of the typical Calvinist, who is interested in politics, but not for the sake of the State; in industry, but not for the sake of wealth. In this and most other ways Calvinism is Christianised Stoicism.

Could the Christian spirit live in a society based on trade and commerce? Calvin thought it was possible, if all luxurious expenditure were rigorously forbidden, and close supervision were exercised to stop all exploitation, fraud, and trickery. The rich were not allowed to live in idleness. In this way Calvinism favoured a kind of ethical Christian Socialism, and was far more successful in founding a Christian society on modern lines than some other attempts that have been made.

The temptation which corrupted the religion of many Calvinists was the natural result of the double doctrine that productive enterprise was the typical godly life, and that almost all ways of spending money were wrong. By acting on these two principles the Calvinistic nations became very rich. By degrees the religious obligations began to fall away, and the habits of industry, which for Calvin had been a religious discipline,

were maintained as a means of making
money. In America and Scotland the older
type may still be met with, but as a rule
neo-Calvinism is not ascetic. If the money-
spinner himself lives hardly, his wife, with
his approval, spends enough for two. She is
a walking advertisement of her husband's
success. Modern ways of making a fortune
are often very different from anything that
Calvin had to deal with at Geneva.

The transition stage may be illustrated by
the following quotation from Baxter. 'If
God show you a way in which you may law-
fully get more than in another way, without
wrong to your soul or to any other, if you
refuse this and choose the less gainful way,
you cross one of the ends of your calling,
and you refuse to be God's steward.' When
this false standard of success has once been
adopted, it is inevitable that 'lawful' means
of making money should come to include
less and less scrupulous methods, till we
reach such caricatures of Christian morality
as are illustrated by Mr. Bulstrode in *Middle-
march*, or in the exhortation of an American
divine, 'Be Christians, and you will be successful.' Lippmann writes: 'The sponsors of

the Broadway Temple in New York City
put the matter in a thoroughly modern,
even if it was in a rather coarse, way when
they proclaimed a campaign to sell bonds as
a five per cent. investment in your fellow
man's salvation. Broadway Temple is to be a
combination of church and skyscraper, religion and revenue, salvation and five per
cent.; and the five per cent. is based on
ethical Christian grounds. The five per cent.,
they hastened to add, was also based on a
gilt-edged real estate mortgage; the salvation
was, we may suppose, a speculative profit.'
The object of putting a church on the top
of a skyscraper is that in New York the
whole building is free from rates.

The ascendancy of the middle class, which
was established in France by the Revolution,
and in England by a slow and peaceable
evolution, favoured an ideal of the godly life
which at its best resembled that of Calvin.
The good man was a model citizen in an
industrial community. The stainless reputa-
tion of the unmarried woman in the last
century was taken for granted, and adultery
was condemned as disgraceful.

The agrarian and industrial revolutions

(the word is perhaps not very appropriate) uprooted a large part of the population from its traditional environment, and while the country was fighting for its life against Napoleon it was impossible for Parliament to pay much attention to what Carlyle called the condition of England question. After the war it gradually became plain that England was to enjoy a spell of great prosperity as the workshop of the world. Large fortunes were made in business, and the rewards of business enterprise were so great (as they were more recently in America) that ambitious men were strongly attracted to what the Greeks called the chrematistic career. The early Victorian men of business, of whom Bright and Cobden were types, were conscientious men, and not snobs. They had no wish to imitate either the manners or the morals of the aristocracy. Some of them supported, others opposed the laws which were introduced at this time to alleviate the hardships of the wage-earners. When competition is keen, it is almost impossible for an individual employer to be very generous. The masters were convinced that in building up their businesses they were doing their duty in the state of life to which they had been called, and that their industry and thrift were increasing the well-being of the nation at large. In that period of expansion they were justified in thinking so, though in their opposition to the corn-laws they did not realise the possible consequences of sacrificing the interests of agriculture to those of the industrial towns. This did not become plain till after 1875.

'The benign and wise Disposer of all things, who obliges men, whether they will or not, in pursuing their own selfish interests, to connect the general good with their own individual success.' So Burke rather crudely summed up the philosophy of his generation, a philosophy based on the naïve acceptance of evolutionary optimism. The doctrine of human perfectibility was no invention of industrialists; it was a dream of the eighteenth century *philosophes* in France. But there was much in the amazing triumphs of production which seemed to justify it. It was said in 1830 that whereas two centuries before not one person in a thousand wore stockings, now not one person in a thousand is without them. No one then had any suspicion that the stockings might one day be made in Japan. Production for mass consumption, and not to supply luxuries for the rich, was a new thing and surely a good thing; the small consumer was the chief gainer. The poor were now able to enjoy comforts which the rich in other times could not obtain. The great fortunes of the manufacturers were derived from cheap commodities which were supplied in masses to the small consumer. If the condition of the working class had been as bad as it is often represented, production on this large scale would have been as impossible as in the crowded lands of Asia, where extreme poverty is universal.

And yet the ugliness and ruthlessness of early Victorian society bore witness to the blunder of sacrificing the higher values to the increase of wealth and population. The whole episode which made England the workshop of the world was alien to the spirit and the character of the English people. The weary Titan, with labour-dimmed eyes, staggering on to his goal, is not the real John Bull. We have never been a nation of shop-keepers; we are rather bad shop-keepers; we

have neither the penurious thriftiness of the
French nor the laborious diligence of the
German. Like the other peoples of north-
western Europe we have always insisted on
being well fed, and beyond all other nations
we have been devoted to sport and games.
Besides this, our literature shows that there
is in the English character a vein of lofty
idealism, which has inspired most of our
great poets.

The industrial struggle went on after the
enthusiasm which had marked its earlier
stages had evaporated, because a dense population had been brought into existence,
which could be kept from starvation only by
foreign trade. The machine continued to
work, but with increasing dissatisfaction on
the part of its servants.

But the results of industrialism had before
this been denounced by almost all the great
writers of the period. Carlyle in *Sartor Resartus*, and Tennyson in *Maud*, had tried to
find some spiritual values in the new society;
but both were completely disillusionised before they died. Carlyle hates political economy, 'the dismal science', and with all his
contempt for the Catholic revival he casts

151

wistful eyes on his vision of society in the middle ages. Mass-production has led to mass-thinking and loss of liberty. Mill foresees that machine-made mediocrity will take the place of the vigorous individualism of the national character. Froude says that where money is the measure of worth, the wrong persons are always uppermost. Ruskin, who was far more in sympathy with romanticism than Carlyle, insists that to identify money with wealth is barbarous. He was one of the first to realise that to rely on competition for employment among the labourers as a means to secure good and cheap labour was a mistake. The quality of the work would deteriorate. Ruskin's Tory socialism often recalls Plato, whose dialogues were like a second Bible to him. Charles Reade, who fully realised the strength of the workers' case, was horrified by the tyranny and brutality of the trade unions in 1870. Such results were to be expected when the human costs of productive industry had so long been ignored.

All these writers—and we may add the names of Dickens, Morris, Matthew Arnold, Mrs. Gaskell and Charles Kingsley, protested from different points of view against the in-

humanity and barbarism of making economic efficiency the sole measure of social progress. Their object was to substitute a truer
standard of values for the harsh puritanical
ideal which justified the conduct of the employers to themselves. The cash-nexus, as
Carlyle said, should not be the only bond
which holds society together, and the best
things in human life are not those in which
one man's gain is another man's loss.

That these lessons are being partially
learnt in our own generation is part of the
thesis of this chapter. But we have now to
consider the activities of those who accepted
the economic interpretation of history and
the materialistic standard of value, but
turned them against the employers and the
owners of property. Socialism and Communism belong to the same circle of ideas
as acquisitive Capitalism. Both regard the
possession of money and the things which
money can buy as the supreme good. Both
are out of date as soon as a different standard
is accepted. I shall argue that though the fact
is still imperfectly realised, these idols of the
nineteenth century have in truth been thrown
down from their pedestals, and that this fate

has overtaken the *pleonexia* not only of
Capitalists but of Socialists and Communists.
This does not mean either that private
Capitalism as a social system has failed, or
that State Capitalism as organised in Russia
and other totalitarian States must everywhere lead to economic disaster. Neither of
these is true. Private Capitalism has won re-
sounding successes; the evils which have
accompanied it are to a large extent remedi-
able by legislation without social revolution,
and are mainly due to the one-sided 'economism' which is the subject of this chapter.
On the other hand, State Capitalism is
workable, but only on condition that all
liberty is destroyed. The objections to it are
not primarily economic. But it is extremely
doubtful whether an army of bureaucrats,
exempted by terrorism from outside criticism, would have either the capacity or the
honesty to administer the industrial life of
a highly organised community. Such experiments are most likely to succeed in a backward nation like Russia, which has been
only superficially industrialised. It has yet
to be proved that they can be successful in
Germany, and few men of business in

Britain or the United States would think that anything less than general ruin could result from handing over all large-scale business to government officials. Something of the kind was tried during the Great War, and it was often said that no private firm could have escaped bankruptcy for a month if its affairs were conducted with such reckless ineptitude as the financing of the war under Lloyd George.

But my object in this chapter is to show the disintegrating effects of a wrong standard of values upon the national life. It was not to be expected that the materialistic interpretation of social problems should remain the prerogative of employers of labour. It was not to be expected that employers should be allowed to combine for their own advantage while the labourers were prevented from doing so. Trade Unionism, Socialism, and Communism were the logical application of the same principles which the employers accepted and practised. The interests of Capital and Labour were not identical. The theory of the optimists broke down, and savage class-conflicts were the result.

155

It would not be necessary in this book to expose the economic fallacies of Karl Marx, whose real name was Mordecai. This has been done by many experts in political economy, who are far better equipped for the task than I am. Comparatively few among the numbers who call themselves Marxists have waded through the confused and dreary pages of *Das Kapital*, which H. G. Wells calls a monument of pretentious pedantry. The man has become a cult-hero, whose utterances it is impious to criticise. Like many other Jews, he was a fierce hater, with a strong bent towards apocalyptic beliefs. He never doubted that his dreams were coming true, and soon; but like other determinists he was far from taking the quietistic attitude which might seem natural to those who believe that the millennium will arrive without human effort. Nor is it logical, if the existing state of things, like that which is to follow it, is the inevitable result of natural laws, to feel a furious hatred against the representatives of the contemporary phase of evolution. But intense hatred, though it inspires men to demoniac energy, blinds their eyes to the course which events are taking. So far from it being true that wealth was certain to be concentrated in fewer and fewer hands, the nineteenth century saw the creation of an enormous middle class, with interests in both camps, and a progressive improvement in the economic condition of the wage-earner. That these changes were largely the result of legislation promoted by humanitarian reformers only filled the minds of Marxists with detestation of all schemes of social amelioration. As for the prediction that after the revolution the State would 'wither away', events have proved that the sequel of social revolution on Socialist lines is such tyranny as the world has never seen before.

A ship's crew, sailing over an uncharted sea and doubtful of their direction, would hardly choose as their captain a man who believed in wrecks as a principle. But the leaders of Socialism and Communism are wreckers, as they avow themselves. A few quotations from their utterances will put the matter beyond doubt. The purpose of the revolutionists is 'to render impossible the present means of production. The miner's object is to paralyse the mine when and as he pleases.' (G. D. H. Cole.) 'To do good work for a capitalist employer is merely to help a thief to steal more successfully.' (The same.) 'The workers have the right to use every method likely to weaken the power of their employers.' (W. Mellor.) [1] 'In the class war all weapons are justifiable.' 'The object of all organisation among the workers is to be able to stop production.' (W. Mellor.) 'The great weapon of the workers against their masters is disorder. It is the great value of the General Strike that it overturns Society absolutely.' 'Although it is not as a rule wise to offer physical violence to blacklegs, there is nothing wrong

[1] 'The following table', says Professor Hearnshaw, 'is damnatory. It explains not only the depression of the coal trade but much of the adversity of all industries dependent upon coal.

Year.	Output per person per annum.	Wage-cost of Output.
1888	299 tons	52
1898	282 ,,	60
1908	248 ,,	91
1918	224 ,,	197

'In America the wage-cost is about seven shillings a ton. How is it possible for British industry to hold its own in the markets of the world?'

about it except in the eyes of the law and the middle classes.' 'Punctuality, regularity, discipline, industry, are a set of slave virtues.' (G. D. H. Cole.)

It is not surprising that in order to induce the working men to swallow this deadly poison, which would wreck any association of men and women coming together for the common good, it is necessary to tear up religion by the roots. 'The idea of God is the keystone of a perverted civilisation.' (Marx.) 'Christianity and Socialism stand towards each other as fire and water.' (Bebel.) 'To suppress religion, which provides an illusory happiness, is to establish the claim of real happiness.' (*Nouveau Parti*, 1884.) 'The revolution denies religion altogether.' (Bebel.) 'The first word of religion is a lie.' (Engels.) 'Christian doctrine is more revolting to the higher moral sense of to-day than the Saturnalia or the cult of Proserpina could have been to the conscience of the early Christians.' (Belfort Bax.)

Most of these utterances, which for pure Satanism and cowardly treason surpass anything heard in the world before, are the voices of armchair philosophers who, we

159

may expect, would be among the early victims of a real revolution. But we have only
to look at Russia and Spain to see that in
countries where the rich and poor have
stood opposed to each other, with only a
small and weak middle class to mediate between them, these prophets have been taken
at their word. The excesses of the French
Revolution, which horrified our ancestors
at the end of the eighteenth century, fade
into insignificance beside the wholesale
butcheries in Russia, and also at Madrid and
Barcelona. One section of the community
has declared a war of extermination against
the rest, and has found in the writings of the
intelligentsia ample warrant for its worst
crimes.

That the social order has after all not been
subverted, except where industrialism was
very weak, is in part a testimony to the inherent strength of a system which its enemies are trying to destroy by every kind of
sabotage, and in this country to the good
sense and moderation of the British working
men themselves, who, as Bernard Shaw says,
have never really been touched by Communism.

The quotations which I have given are all taken from publications at least twenty years old; I have done this on purpose. One of the authors would now express himself less truculently.[1] His case illustrates the point which I am trying to make, namely, that the bitter antagonism of classes which was caused by concentrating attention solely upon getting and spending money is now dying down. A good example of the change is furnished by Galsworthy's plays and novels. In his earlier works he showed a deep indignation at social injustice and at the entire want of comprehension which prevented employers and employed from understanding each other. During the Great

---

[1] Hearnshaw, *A Survey of Socialism* (1929), gives the following quotations from Mr. Cole's writings. 'Collectivism is at best only the sordid dream of a business man with a conscience.' 'It is intellectually bankrupt.' 'It is a Prussianising movement, which inevitably leads to administrative tyranny.' Collectivists are 'either knaves who hate freedom, or fools who do not know what freedom means.' 'In plain terms, the Communist Party is a failure; the I.L.P. is played out; the S.D.F. is a mere haven of refuge for socialists ill at ease in other groups; the Fabian Society is a mere table-rapping voice from the dead; and the Guild-Socialist movement almost non-existent as an effective force.' The idols are indeed fallen when a former champion of Fabianism can so express himself.

War he wrote: 'If we really want to extrac
from the furnace of this fearful conflagra
tion some gold of comfort, we shall see to i
that we do not go back to the deadlock o
futile and bitter strife which was paralysin
the country's soul.' But in the early years o
the century he had not seen any way in
which these relations could be humanised
During and after the war he felt more hope
ful, and was conscious of a new inspiration
He resuscitated his puppets, the Forsyte
family, and described the children and grand
children of the old acquisitive Forsytes. In
stead of idealising Soames' wife Irene, surely
one of the worst cads in fiction, he makes u
sympathise with old Soames, who is con
fronted with the new generation, pleasure
loving and contemptuous of moral and
social inhibitions, but free from the hard
unsympathetic standards of moribund puri
tanism. Soames represents a lost cause, the
ideals of the middle class in the later nine
teenth century. Galsworthy was no longer
fighting against these ideals; he can do justice
to those who lived by them, and he deplores
the aimlessness and frivolity of post-war
society.

162

Another book which illustrates the change is the late E. F. Benson's *As We Are*. He describes the moral downfall of an aristocratic family which, like many in real life, had kept contemptuously aloof from the vulgarities of the Edwardian smart set, but which in the next generation succumbed to the post-war dissolution of all traditions. This is another aspect of the bloodless revolution which was hastened and partly caused by the Great War. The class which Benson describes will undoubtedly be extinguished by the events which are now in progress.

It is significant that this toleration and sympathy are not apparent in writers who began life amid hard struggles caused by poverty, unlike the two just mentioned, who belonged to the prosperous professional class. Dickens, though he was too fond of money, never understood the class into which his talents had raised him, and there is no sign that either Bernard Shaw or H. G. Wells feels any regret for the social order which war and predatory taxation are destroying.

Those who had opportunities of observing

163

the life of aristocrats and plutocrats before and after the Great War must have been struck by the good humour and equanimity with which the spoilt children of fortune accepted the enforced change in their habits brought about by that catastrophe. If they did not exactly 'take joyfully the spoiling of their goods', they did not squeal over the loss of half their incomes. It was plain that they had no thought of putting up a fight against a system which had deprived them of effective representation and was now gradually reducing them to what their fathers would have called genteel poverty. More than one great lady has said to me, 'We were too well off before the war.' When I said to another that I wished I had been born fifty years earlier, she replied, 'I do not. Think of all the state which my grandparents had to keep up.' It seemed that they were not much attached to the luxury to which they had been accustomed. Some of the younger ones wished for all the pleasure they could get, and above all for varied experience and what they would have called self-expression; but they had little taste for the ostentation and exclusiveness of Victorian society.

164

This change has now gone much further. The recklessness of the ten years which followed the war has now subsided. It was an ugly episode in our social history, which has had parallels after other wars. But there has been no return to the prudential maxims of the middle class. Our young people—I am speaking mainly of families in my own station of life—are curiously indifferent to money and comfort. They marry cheerfully on a bungalow and a baby Austin. The wives do all the household work themselves, and are much better cooks than the workman's wife. They would laugh at the idea that they ought to save one-third of their incomes. Even the successful man knows that taxation makes it impossible to 'found a family', and thus the main inducement to acquire wealth no longer exists. A few rich men live luxuriously on the principle, 'let us eat and drink, for to-morrow we die.' They would rather throw their money into the sea than save it to be confiscated by politicians to bribe the electorate. But very few fortunes are now made, and the life of business becomes less and less attractive. The prosperity of this country really culminated before the end of the last century, though the fact was not admitted at first. We must now submit to progressively diminishing returns. The golden age has passed, never to return.

The decay of economism is shown in other ways. When the Great War broke out, it was widely believed that the 'workers of the world' would 'unite' in refusing to take part in it. They would seize the opportunity to combine with the proletariat in enemy countries to overthrow capitalism. This expectation was completely erroneous. In every country the socialist revolutionary movement collapsed at the call to arms. The upper and middle classes, who knew that war would wholly or partially ruin them, voted for it without hesitation. One of the first to see the significance of this was Mussolini. The collapse of the German communists and social democrats when Hitler seized the power was almost ludicrous. For Hitler did not overthrow a tottering government, but a well-organised constitution, which was functioning fairly well. It had failed to heal the wounds which German national pride received in 1919, and when

the flag of militant nationalism was un-
furled, all the idols of the last century,
liberty, democracy, pacifism, socialism, and
communism, were broken and cast aside
without a struggle. I am not suggesting that
the change was for the better, but it does
mean that private acquisitiveness and materialism are no longer dominant ideas with the
young.

Continental observers have noticed the
emergence of a new type, hard, cruel,
ruthless, but well disciplined and in a strange
way idealistic. These are the men who keep
the new dictatorships in being. They are to
be seen everywhere in Russia, in Germany,
and in Italy. This type hardly exists at present in England or France. The new 'chauf-
feur-type', glorified by Shaw and Wells, is
realistic but not savage. The great danger
both in France and England is the enormous
multiplication of small State officials. The
service of the State, though not lucrative
except at the top, gives security and the
modicum of power which is pleasant to
Jacks-in-office. The system is terribly expensive, and it does not seem to promote efficiency. But it is likely that a steadily in-

creasing part of the national income will go in supporting a horde of little bureaucrats, ignorant, indolent, and insolent.

The ideal of economic equality—the artificial equalisation of unequals—is by no means self-evident on grounds of justice, and the type of society which it would produce is most repellent. Nor, human nature being what it is, would it last long. It has long been a utopian dream; but its popularity in our day may be ascribed to three causes—the over-estimation of the importance of money as a means to happiness, the decay of the hierarchical organisation of society, which had been held to justify a degree of magnificence in the ruling class, and the transfer of political power to the most numerous and poorest part of the population. Of these the first is in process of being remedied by a change in the accepted standard of values. The second change is almost complete, since feudalism has abdicated, and the 'leisured class' which succeeded it is no longer respected even by itself. We are amused to think that a hundred years ago a gentleman often meant a man who was not obliged to earn his living. The third is the inevitable

168

result of democracy, and will continue to operate in the progressive spoliation of the unrepresented minority. This is really, as I have said, a substitute for socialism, which will prevent the establishment of collectivism except on a limited scale; for the abolition of private property would dry up the source which supplies the enormous sum spent every year on 'social services'. In the near future the tax-paying class will not be entirely extinguished; it will continue to exist as a milch cow shorn of all superfluities. The simple life will perforce be accepted, and technological improvements will make it tolerable.

Moralists in the past were fond of inveighing against the evils of luxury, and Tocqueville [1] goes so far as to say that comfort is more insidious than luxury. It is doubtful whether the future really belongs to the high standard nations, who show their fear of cheap labour by excluding Asiatics from their territories by force. It is the nations who have most to lose who cripple themselves by armaments and pre-

[1] A Frenchman tells me that 'de' Tocqueville, almost universal in English writers, is incorrect.

ventive wars. From this point of view we may perhaps hope that the uses of adversity may be sweet, though they can hardly be sweetening.

But the spiritual capital of a nation consists in its beliefs, hopes, interests, and affections. Its spiritual income is the use made of these. One might even say that spiritual wealth alone exists as an aggregate, because so much of material wealth perishes in conflict. The only way to increase the real public wealth is by the creation of new values. Religion, high character, and culture enhance and create values everywhere. Selfishness and hatred, envy and discontent destroy values to an enormous extent for those who indulge them. They cannot enjoy what they have, and they poison the air around them. The simple maxim that love is the fulfilling of the law is sound economics as well as sound morality. Sowers of hatred are the worst public enemies.

IV
PACIFISM

IV

PACIFISM

War, 'a method of contest by violence', as Cicero defines it, seems to have arisen in the bronze age. Man, whom Nature has furnished with only such poor weapons as his teeth and fists, was slow to interfere much with his own species till he had provided himself with suitable tools. From that time to this his ferocity towards his own kind has been a byword and the scandal of creation.

What should be the attitude of a Christian towards war? This question, which at first sight seems simple, is in reality exceedingly difficult, as is proved by the vacillation of the Christian Churches from the first centuries of our era to the present time.

The message of the angel of the Nativity was 'Peace on earth and good will to men', or 'peace to men of good will'. Christ came to earth to put an end to strife and violence. His own words leave no room for doubt. 'Blessed are the peacemakers, for they shall be called the children of God.' 'I say unto you, love your enemies; bless them that hate you; pray for them that despitefully use you and persecute you.' 'Resist not him that is evil.' 'Put up thy sword, for they that take the sword shall perish by the sword.' 'If my kingdom were of this world, then would my servants fight; but my kingdom is not from hence.'

St. Paul interprets the teaching of the Master correctly. There is to be no strife among men, because our enemies are not flesh and blood, but 'spiritual wickedness in the heavenly places'—the supernatural powers of evil. In Christ there is neither Jew nor Greek, barbarian, Scythian, bond nor free; we are all one man in Christ Jesus. 'Whence come wars and fightings among you?' asks the writer of the Epistle of James. 'Even from the lusts that war in your members.' 'The wrath of man worketh not the righteousness of God.'

The only book of the New Testament which shows a different spirit is the Apocalypse, which was admitted into the Canon after much hesitation. It belongs, in part at least, to the literature of Jewish apocalyptic, and breathes the traditional hatred of the Jews to Rome.

Two or three misunderstandings must be removed. Christ said, 'Think ye that I am come to bring peace on earth? I came not to bring peace, but a sword.' This is the Hebrew idiom, which does not distinguish between intention and effect. No one can suppose that Christ *wished* to bring war upon earth, but He foresaw that men will die and kill for their deepest convictions.

He uses military metaphors and similes. This does not prove that He sanctioned war. He compares the unexpected coming of the Kingdom of God to that of a housebreaker, without meaning to express approval of burglary.

It is not true that the use of the word ἐχθρὸς for 'enemy' shows that only private feuds are forbidden. The classical word for a public enemy (πολέμιος—the Latin *hostis* as opposed to *inimicus*) does not occur in biblical Greek.

It is more to the point to ask whether the law of non-resistance was meant to be taken literally. Like other moral teachers, Christ employed the method of hyperbole. There

175

are even some formal contradictions in His words, the solution of which is left to the common sense of His hearers. He was not a legislator; He lays down general principles, the application of which often raises problems for societies where conditions are quite unlike those which He envisaged in instructing Galilean peasants. The principle of non-resistance was laid down for a little flock in a hostile environment. It was faithfully followed by the apostolic and post-apostolic Church, which even under persecution never encouraged a political rising. But an organised society cannot abstain from the use of coercion. No one would suggest that a Christian government must not suppress a gang of criminals within its own borders; and if this is admitted, can we doubt that it should defend itself against an invading enemy? Does the precept, 'resist not the evil man' mean that the Poles were wrong in resisting the Germans, and the Finns the Russians? Even though the independence of those peoples was only twenty years old, so that the invaders could claim that they were only recovering their own, I cannot think, especially when we remember the barbarous

176

conduct of the invaders, that in these cases armed resistance was contrary to the law of Christ. Nevertheless, we have here made a concession which complicates the problem. We must, I think, fall back on the doctrine of natural rights, which has always been accepted by the Church. These rights include the right to life, liberty, and the enjoyment of property honestly come by and conscientiously used.

The law of love forbids war absolutely. But a purely predatory State, like the Assyrians or the Tartars, has put itself outside the comity of civilised humanity. To acquiesce in pillage, massacre, and outrage is to encourage in crime those who acknowledge no moral sanctions.

The Fathers of the Church, before the concordat with the civil government under Constantine, are almost unanimous in condemning war without any compromise. But there seem to have been Christians in the army in the time of Tertullian, and there were certainly many among the troops led by Constantine. The lost work of Celsus, written late in the second century, contained an earnest appeal to the Christians not to leave the empire to the fate which was already beginning to threaten it. But the imperial government had done nothing to win the loyalty of the Christians, who were only human, and naturally resented being tortured and thrown to the lions in the amphitheatre. With some exceptions they were not interested in preserving the classical culture. As long as they were treated as enemy aliens, they saw no reason to modify the teaching of Christ as inculcating pure pacifism.

After Constantine the tone of the Church changes. It was part of the concordat that it should support the civil government. Ambrose appeals to the Old Testament. And here it may be said that though the later books of the Old Testament are full of beautiful visions of a happy time when wars shall cease in all the world, and when even the beasts shall no longer prey upon each other, the narratives of the ferocious wars of the Israelites have had a most unfortunate influence upon Christian theory and practice. Ulphilas, the apostle of the Goths, withheld these books from his pugnacious converts; the Anglican missionaries to the

178

Maoris were embarrassed by them. There is an amazing sermon by Cardinal Newman justifying the massacres of the Canaanites by the Hebrews. Calvin at Geneva and the Puritans in the time of Cromwell confidently appealed to these examples.

Augustine, whose teaching largely determined that of western Catholicism, held that war is justified in repelling wanton and rapacious attacks, and that in preventing such crimes we are acting in the true interest of the aggressor. By leaving him unpunished '*nutritur immunitas, et mala voluntas velut hostis interior roboratur*'. And again, 'Without justice what is empire but brigandage on a large scale?'

With Martin Luther we come to that ruinous dualism of public and private ethics, already accepted by Machiavelli, which has been widely adopted in Germany, and which by openly proclaiming that the teaching of Christ has no reference to the conduct of States has made modern Europe a hell upon earth.

The Christian conscience has never been at its ease about any of these concessions. Ought we to accept the solution advocated

179

first by the Stoics, that besides the absolute
law of nature, which would operate in a sinless world, there is a relative law of nature,
which we must accept in our fallen condition? The great Church looked the facts in
the face and made concessions; some of the
sects would make none. Among these, who
included the Doukhobors in Russia and the
Mennonites in the Low Countries, the most
notable were the Quakers. 'Whoever can
reconcile "Resist not evil",' says Barclay
one of their leaders, 'with Resist evil by
force; again, "Give also thy other cheek"
with Strike again; "Love thine enemies"
with Spoil them, make a prey of them, pur-
sue them with fire and sword; or "Pray for
those that persecute you" with Persecute
them with fines, imprisonment, and death
itself; whoever can find a means to reconcile
these things, may be supposed also to have
found a way to reconcile God with the Devil
Christ with Antichrist, light with darkness
and good with evil.' Tolstoi in our day has
taken the same line with a thoroughness
characteristic of his race.

Rejecting this extreme view, which would
leave justice disarmed and helpless, and

allowing that circumstances may arise which make a defensive war inevitable, have we found a principle which will guide us in concrete cases? Let us try to answer in several typical instances.

Was the conquest of North and South America by the white man justifiable? Where the indigenous population consisted of nomad hunters, they could hardly be said to be in occupation of a great continent. We may say that European colonisation was justifiable, but that the extermination of the Indians in parts of the United States was not. The case of the Aztec empire is more doubtful, since there the Spaniards found a settled civilisation of a sort; but we cannot give a high place to a people who were constantly at war, and who practised cannibalism and human sacrifice. However, the reduction of the natives to serfdom, from which they are only now escaping, was unjust. The conquest of Peru by Pizarro cannot be justified, for the Peruvians were relatively humane, and their State-socialism was an interesting experiment.

Ought we to have left Australia to the Blackfellows? No; these savages were not in effective occupation of the continent. But we need not have exterminated the Tasmanians.

Which of the major wars waged by Great Britain can be justified? The invasions of France in the Hundred Years' War were clearly unjustifiable. So was the opium war with China. So was the Crimean War. Several other great wars, including the war against Napoleon, were intended to restore the balance of power in Europe, which was threatened by some continental nation. In defence of this principle we have fought against Louis XIV, Napoleon, Nicholas I, Wilhelm II, and now against Hitler. This at least is how we are judged on the Continent. Our own theory is that we are high-minded but rather stupid. We are devoted to peace, but occasionally our righteous indignation at the treatment of a weak nation by a strong compels us to draw the sword in the cause of right against wrong. We are in favour of disarmament. We should like to see continental nations beat their swords into plough-shares; but when it is suggested that Britannia should beat her trident into a toasting-fork, that is a rather different thing.

'The dread of being duped by other nations,' said Bentham, 'the notion that foreign heads are more able, though at the same time foreign hearts are less honest than our own, has always been one of our prevailing weaknesses.' Foreigners do not credit us with being either stupid or disinterested. We are in favour of peace now, certainly; we are like a gambler who after raking in a huge stake, proposes to play for love for the rest of the evening. Our policy, they think, has been astute and unscrupulous. Our naval supremacy has enabled us to pick up numerous unconsidered trifles in the way of colonies, and we have not consulted the wishes of the natives before taking them. Whenever any continental Power threatens to overtop the rest, we have formed a coalition against it, and have hung on like a bulldog until we have pulled it down. Our pretext for intervention is a hitherto unsuspected affection for some small nation—Portugal, Turkey, Serbia, Abyssinia, Czechoslovakia or Poland.

Which of the two opinions is right, or is the truth somewhere between them? I will not give an opinion, since my own country is concerned.

We may think of other difficult cases. Was Codrington right in destroying the Turko-Egyptian fleet at Navarino in 1827? I think he was. But for our intervention the Greek population of the Morea would have been exterminated, and their place filled by Egyptians and negroes. Our debt to ancient Greece forbade the toleration of such an outrage, and we were able to prevent it without a regular war.

Is a preventive war ever justified? If we have reason to believe that a foreign Power has determined to attack us, may we strike before they are ready? It would be very dangerous to assent to this. Almost all modern wars are begun in fear of attack, sometimes justified fear, sometimes not.

Is the desire to find room for surplus population a sound reason for war? I cannot admit that an unregulated birth-rate gives a nation the right to encroach on its neighbours, and it is more than probable that the land which is coveted for colonisation is peopled already. The Germans, as it happens, do not need more *Lebensraum*. Their birth-rate, when compared with their corrected death-rate, only just reaches parity.

184

Lastly, what are we to say of ideological wars? Were the Crusaders justified in trying to recover the Holy Sepulchre? What is our verdict about the wars of religion? Are the new dictatorships so hateful that they ought not to be tolerated? Without saying that such wars are never justifiable, it is very rare that one nation has a right to deprive another of the government which for the time it prefers; and in most cases the plea is dishonest. Wars in support of rebellions in another country are seldom successful, and only increase the dislocation of society in the nation engaged in civil war.

The burden of proof always lies with the nation which chooses war, and the reasons alleged are generally, in part at least, hypocritical.

That war is the greatest evil in human life, and that no good can ever come of it, are in my opinion certain. In the eighteenth century, when war was far more humane than it is now, there is a striking passage in 'Thoughts on the late Transactions respecting Falkland's Islands,' (1771). 'The life of a modern soldier is ill represented in heroick fiction. War has means of destruction more

185

formidable than the cannon and the sword. Of the thousands and ten thousands that perished in our late contest with France and Spain, a very small part ever felt the stroke of an enemy; the rest languished in tents and ships amidst damp and putrefaction; pale, torpid, spiritless and helpless; gasping and groaning unpitied among men made obdurate by long continuance of hopeless misery, and whelmed in pits or heaved into the ocean without notice and without remembrance. By incommodious encampments and unwholesome stations where courage is useless and enterprise impracticable, fleets are silently dispeopled, and armies sluggishly melted away.' 'Take my word for it,' said the Duke of Wellington, 'if you had seen but one day of war you would pray to Almighty God that you might never again see an hour of war.' 'War', said Channing, 'is the concentration of all human crimes.' 'The present state of Europe', said Lord Avebury, 'is a disgrace to us, not only as men of common sense, but as being incompatible with any form of religious conviction.'

The horrors of war have been enormously augmented in the present century. The creed of nationalism makes whole nations belligerents; there is no longer any distinction between combatants and non-combatants. All the old chivalrous conventions have been discarded. The invention of flying has so far been a curse to humanity. It is a law that when the defence is stronger than the attack, wars are less frequent and less destructive. Apart from warfare in the air, the defence perhaps has now the advantage. But in the air the attack is so much stronger than the defence that nations are deterred, if at all, from bombing raids upon enemy towns only by fear of retaliation. It is very doubtful whether any capital can be protected against attacks from the air. That civilised peoples should be compelled to revert to the habits of burrowing animals and cave-dwellers is a disgrace which would be ludicrous if it were not tragic.

In the Crimean War Dundonald suggested the use of sulphur fumes against Sebastopol. The War Office refused on the ground that 'an operation of this nature would contravene the laws of civilised warfare.' Far more poisonous gases than sulphur were used in the Great War, first by the

Germans, and then by all the belligerents. To the credit of both sides they were not used in Spain. In 1925 the Powers at Geneva signed a protocol entirely forbidding the use of gas in warfare. Like other pacts, this was treated as a scrap of paper.

What devilish discoveries have been made since 1918 will perhaps be revealed before long. The gases used in the Great War were:

Chlorine, which injures the lungs.

Chloropicrine, which attacks the eyes and lungs. Phosgene is similar, but even more poisonous.

Mustard gas, which poisons the ground for days or even weeks. It causes blindness, blistered skin, bronchitis and pneumonia.

Lewisite, made more poisonous by arsenic. It has been calculated that 5,000 pounds of Lewisite could poison an area fifty miles long and thirty-five miles wide.

Thermite is for incendiary bombs. It rises to a temperature nearly as hot as the sun's surface; water cannot extinguish it.

There has been nothing like this in the history of the world. Europe is becoming a cooperative suicide club.

The horror of war has found eloquent

expression at all times and in all literatures.
It would be strange if it were not so. But
mention must be made of a book which
created a great sensation over the whole of
the civilised world, (Sir) Norman Angell's
The Great Illusion, published in 1910, four
years before the outbreak of the Great War.
The economic interpretation of history, as
I have said elsewhere in this book, is now
very popular; it has inspired Marxism and
other movements. Angell undertakes to
prove that even if we put aside, as he does
almost ostentatiously, all moral, humanitarian, and religious considerations, war is a
monstrous absurdity, an egregious miscalcu-
lation on the part of any nation which ima-
gines that its material interests can be thereby promoted. In this attempt he is quite
successful, at least as regards wars between
nations on the same plane of civilisation.
Even Bismarck's shrewdly calculated wars are
not really an exception. A war of extermination waged by a civilised nation in need of
more territory against helpless savages must
be judged on other grounds. But the verdict
of events has been that the economic interpretation of history is erroneous. Human

conduct is actually determined by other and stronger motives than loss and gain.

Last year we had ample opportunities of forming an opinion on the real impulses and springs of action, we can hardly call them reasons, which produce the war-mentality. My own experience has been almost entirely with members of my own social group, that is to say with men and women who must look forward, as the result of the present war, to see almost everything that they care for in the world destroyed—their savings confiscated or reduced to nothing by inflation, their husbands, sons and brothers sent to the shambles, and the social order in which they have lived happily enough brought to an end. One might have thought that these considerations, reinforced in some cases by their belief in Christianity, would have been enough to arouse a very strong resistance to the war-mongers. It has not been so. Those who have everything to lose and nothing to gain by war are, if we may judge by their vocal spokesmen, supporters of the Government, which is also backed up by the large majority of Socialists, including the author of *The Great Illusion*, who until

190

ately were believed to carry their pacifism
o the verge of anti-patriotism. The defection
f this large party from the support of peace
1as been a shock to some who believed that
n international affairs at any rate they could
be relied on to oppose violence. The explana-
ion is not very simple. The Government
loes not dare to ask the working class to
nake serious sacrifices, with the important
exception that their younger members are
required to risk their lives in the trenches.
Their motives, I think, are largely ideological. They have been taught that Fascism is
a counter-revolutionary movement, while
the Bolsheviks are the advance-guard of their
own party. As they have been callous about
the hideous cruelties of the Communists,
they are not likely to be as much moved as
their grandparents would have been by the
barbarities of Nazism; but they realise that
Fascism is an enemy of democracy, that is to
say, of the domination of the country by
their own class.

The position of the war-party in my own
station is certainly not ignoble. But when
we consider that war between civilised nations is condemned by common sense and

humanity; that it is a negation of the reli
gion which most of us profess; that its futilit
has been amply demonstrated; [1] that, a
Wellington said, there is nothing worse than
winning a war except losing it; that it in
volves the sacrifice of our dearest affection
and of the objects to which our working live
are directed, must we not suspect that the
exalted motives by which we believe our
selves to be animated are a rationalisation o
deep-seated instincts which have their root
in the unconscious mind, and which, if they
were realised for what they are, might no
receive the sanction either of our conscience
or of our intelligence?

The influence of the unconscious mind
upon human action has in my opinion been
worked too hard in recent psychology. It i
acceptable to the philosophy of irrationalism
the spread of which I for one greatly regret
But in the case of war-mentality I can find
no other explanation of the fact that this
destructive evil has not followed into desue
tude such institutions as cannibalism, human

---

[1] We went to war in 1914 with three objects—(1) to
destroy German militarism, (2) to put an end to war.
(3) to make the world safe for democracy.

sacrifice, exposure of infants, and (alas! that I can no longer add) judicial torture. Primitive instincts act powerfully after suggestion, but the stimulus has to be applied. Normally the modern man is not bellicose, but he can be easily roused to irrational fury, if it can be made to appear to him that he is not moved by any private or personal injury, such as would make it his duty to weigh the case dispassionately. In July 1914, no one in England was thinking of war; a month later we were all boiling with rage against the German emperor.

If this diagnosis is correct, the chances of abolishing war by argument may seem to be remote. So I fear they are. But there comes a point where the ruinous consequences of yielding to certain instincts are so undeniable that reason may assert her control. And meanwhile we may consider the different stimuli which excite the instinct of pugnacity into activity. Some at least of these may be avoided.

Group competition arises partly from the acquisitiveness natural to man, and partly from fear of such aggression by other societies. It represses intra-group competition in the same degree as it stimulates rivalry with other groups. Class warfare has been for the time suppressed in the two nations, Germany and Italy, which are organised for struggle against other groups. A group so organised tends to disintegrate when the stimulus of real or supposed external danger is withdrawn. Hence some advocate militarism as a remedy for internal sedition. It is certain that many governments have made war to protect themselves from their own subjects. Madame de Staël wrote: 'Many people think that if Bonaparte had undertaken neither the invasion of Spain nor of Russia he would still be emperor. But he needed war both to establish and preserve absolutism. A great nation would not have endured the monotonous and degrading weight of despotism, if military glory had not continually roused and animated public sentiment.' It has been said that a man may build himself a throne of bayonets, but he cannot sit on it. Other wars are to be accounted for in the same way. Napoleon III knew that Louis Philippe had been deposed because 'France was bored'—bored by peace and bourgeois prosperity. So he determined

o give his subjects excitement and if possible
glory'. The Gauls, it was said two thousand
years ago, care most for two things, soldier-
ng and clever conversation. So 'Napoleon
the Little' went to war in the Crimea, Italy,
Mexico, and ended at Sedan. Nicholas II of
Russia may have thought that war in 1914
gave him his only chance of escaping from
the revolution which seemed to be imminent. None of these experiments ended
happily for their authors. A nation on the
brink of revolution is apt to be beaten; and
even if its people for a time are infected by
war-fever, they will visit their defeat on their
rulers. *Delirant Achivi; plectuntur reges.* The
only final integration is a spiritual one, because only on this plane is there real community of interests.

We have also to take into account the
glorification of war as a noble thing in itself.
This is still the sincere conviction of many
in militarised States such as Germany and
Italy, where utterances of a pacifist tendency
are actually penalised. This cult of the
warrior in civilised Europe can be traced
back to the institution of chivalry, which the
Church decided to annex to its own interests

195

instead of discouraging it. It is also the
Japanese religion of Bushido, a code of
military honour. Even those who regard
this ideal as atavistic and, under modern
conditions, utterly mischievous, cannot fail
to admire the courage, discipline, and self
sacrifice which it evokes. There is something
in the middle-class utopia of peace, industry
and material comfort which fails to satisfy
the whole of human nature. Like Tennyson
in *Maud*, the quiet citizen has been known
to welcome the outbreak of even a Crimean
War.

The same impatience to escape from the
monotony of a prosaic and uninteresting
routine accounts for the eagerness of many
young men to enlist as soon as war breaks
out. Most of them have no strong wish to
kill enemy soldiers; but they feel that they
are summoned to do something worth doing, something better than earning money
for themselves or their employers. A few of
them may develop sadistic instincts under
appropriate stimuli. 'A man of mild manners', says Hume, 'can form no idea of in-
veterate revenge or cruelty;' but the mild
ness of our manners may be due to the ab-

ence of temptation, and may prove to be only skin deep.

Professor William Brown, in his book on the psychology of war, rightly lays stress on the mischievous activities of the newspaper press. 'Whenever there is a mention of an imminent war we have in a certain type of press flaming headlines and excited writing which appeal, and not in vain, to something ancestral within us all. Ought not these newspaper people to be brought to an adequate realisation of their responsibility? They know the truth of things to some extent, although if they knew the whole truth they would no longer be good propagandists.' The newspapers are the worst sinners; but others, including some of my own profession, are strangely forgetful of the precepts of Christianity when their blood is up.

Wars of annexation or exploitation for the capture of raw materials, such as oil and the precious metals, have been undertaken in recent times. The Opposition accused the Rand magnates of provoking the Boer War.

The notion that wars are made by the armament firms is groundless. The shareholders in these companies have no political influence; they are not more wicked than other people; most of them are small investors with many other irons in the fire; they stand to lose much more than they gain by a great war. The interests and therefore the influence of capital are now definitely pacific. The present war will complete the destruction of wealth which the Great War began. A rich American living in London told me that he has to pay 79 per cent. of his income in taxes. 'In America,' he added, 'though America is not at war, I should have to pay 82 per cent. After this war there will be no more rich men in either country.'

I have dealt in another chapter with the romantic patriotism which has produced the fanatical cult of nationalism, the greatest danger to civilisation at the present time. I need add nothing more here, except to say that when I remember the epidemic of chauvinism which swept over England towards the end of the last century, and our complete recovery from it, I see no reason to regard the disease as incurable. H. A. L. Fisher's summary of the German national character is probably as correct as any description of a national character can be. 'A lack of balance and moderation goes with the character of this remarkable people, at once the most virile and enthusiastic, the most industrious and submissive, the most methodical and sentimental in the world.' But to many foreigners Goethe, who was coolly detached from nationalism, remains as much the quintessential German as Shakespeare is the quintessential Englishman. Unhappily, Germany is at present hermetically sealed against hearing the truth.

But one of the chief causes of war remains to be mentioned. In my conversation with Delbrück of Berlin two years before the war I regretted the ill-feeling which existed between our two countries. He replied, 'I do not think that dislike matters much, but where there is fear there is danger.' The plain truth is that the fear is justified. As Theodore Roosevelt said: 'It is idle to make speeches and write essays against this fear, because at present the fear has a real basis. At present each nation has cause for the fear it feels. Each nation has cause to believe that its national life is in peril unless it is able to take the national life of one or more of its foes, or at least hopelessly to cripple that foe.

199

The causes of fear must be removed, or no matter what peace may be patched up to-day, or what new treaties may be negotiated to-morrow, these causes will at some future day bring about the same results, bring about a repetition of the same awful tragedy.' On which we may perhaps suggest that there is one great nation to which these words do not apply. There is one nation which is quite invulnerable, and which is therefore in a favourable position for helping Europe out of its troubles.

I will not discuss such proposed remedies as an international air force, for I do not think any remedy of this kind is practicable. Nothing can save Europe except a return to sanity, and as long as frenzied nationalism and well-grounded fear determine the councils of the nations, the prospects for the future must remain dark and threatening.

Some writers whom I respect have argued that a simple refusal to serve, if made by a large number, would make war impossible. It would of course mean a great many martyrdoms. It is pointed out that this was the only weapon used by the early Christians, and that passive resistance has several times

200

compelled a government to change its policy.
I do not know what to say to this proposal.
The notion of a martyr nation, giving itself
up to injustice and spoliation for the most
sacred of all causes, cannot be dismissed with
contempt. But I cannot share the opinion of
some pacifists that no aggression would be
committed against a great nation which deliberately refused to defend itself. Ruinous
injuries might be inflicted upon such a
nation without actually going to war, and
we have seen absolutely unprovoked aggression by Germany on one helpless nation
after another. The treatment of one really
pacific country—China—by other nations is
not encouraging. Nevertheless, I think the
organisation of peace societies is well worth
while. For after all, the vast majority in
every country hate war and earnestly desire
its total abolition.

This chapter, I am well aware, does not
point very hopefully to any cure for the
worst diseases of civilisation. The private
citizen cannot do much more than take to
heart these words of Edmund Burke: 'It is
our business carefully to cultivate in our
minds, to rear to the utmost vigour and

maturity, every sort of generous and honest feeling that belongs to our nature; to bring the dispositions that are lovely in private life into the service and conduct of the commonwealth; so to be patriots as not to forget that we are gentlemen.'

V
HUMANISM

HUMANISM

Humanism is defined in the Oxford Dictionary as 'any system of thought or action which is concerned with merely human interests (as distinguished from divine) or with those of the human race in general.' Some would object to the implied opposition of 'human' and 'divine' interests; but all humanists would agree that the full development of the capacities of men and women should be the goal of social and political activity. The late Dr. Schiller tried to annex the word as the most expressive name for his variety of pragmatism—a modern version of the canon of Protagoras that 'man is the measure of all things;' but this is an unjustifiable narrowing of a useful word which has long been used in the sense above indicated.

Comte's proposal to deify humanity is a form of Narcissism which could have appeared only in the nineteenth century. When our civilisation looks at itself in a mirror, the image does now appear worthy of worship. But the achievements of our race are certainly marvellous. As Austin Freeman says: 'The change in the relation of man to his environment is indeed astounding. Its recital is that of a fairy romance. The little hairless animal that once crept, naked and forlorn, over the surface of the earth, going warily and timorously amidst its numberless perils, snatching a precarious subsistence from chance scraps picked up on the way; clutching as his choicest possession a chunk of stone or a knotted stick; the sport of the elements; the prey of the larger beasts; homeless and shelterless save for the cavern whose tenancy he disputed with the hyena or the cave-bear; behold him now in all the opulence of his great inheritance of knowledge, lording it over the world through which he once slunk in momentary peril of his life. Less gifted with specialised means than any other animal, he has yet outstripped them all. He burrows into the very bowels of the earth; he traverses its surface at a speed that leaves the fleetest beast as stationary; he follows the leviathan into the depths of the sea; he

206

skims the surface of the ocean more swiftly than the flying-fish; he soars to aerial heights inaccessible to the eagle or the condor.' 'Yes,' said an Indian sage to an Englishman; 'you can do all that, but how to walk on the earth you do not yet know.'

These astonishing achievements have been external. There has been no biological progress since the beginning of history. The scanty remains of the Cro-Magnon race show that there once existed on the earth human beings of higher stature and larger brain-capacity than any race of mankind now living. Such physical changes as are now discernible are degenerative, such as the tendency to lose hair, teeth, and toe-nails. Nature gives nothing for nothing. Even so lately as two thousand five hundred years ago there existed a race—the Greeks— superior to modern man both physically and intellectually. *Homo faber*, the tool-using animal, is no longer the handy man that he once was. We often forget how small is the number of persons who can assimilate, transmit, and augment the treasures of the human mind. Such an extermination of intellectuals as is in progress in Russia and

Germany might, if it were universal, plunge
the world into barbarism again. How many
of those who use the new inventions have
any notion of the mechanisms which they
employ? 'You press the button; we do the
rest.' A nation of button-pressers would be
far more helpless than the savage if left to
their own devices.

Man has not yet proved that he can remain permanently civilised, but it does not
seem to be inevitable that civilisations should
decay. There have been flowering-times and
barren times, catabolic and anabolic periods.
In this chapter we must consider the flowering-time which began at the Renaissance;
the rediscovery of Greece, the birth of humanism, and its chequered fortunes during the
last four centuries.

The bright hopes of the Renaissance were
quenched by the Wars of Religion and the
persecutions which accompanied them. Hope
revived with the growth of toleration, but
was again dashed by the violence which the
new idolatry—State-worship—has brought
upon a demented continent.

The mentality of an epoch, says Whitehead, depends on the view of the world

208

dominant in the educated sections of the population. We might now be tempted to say, the half-educated sections; but no doubt every age seems to take its colour from the dominant preoccupation of the most active minds. Science, aesthetics, ethics, religion—there have been epochs when each one of these has been the main centre of interest.

Since the Renaissance the view of the world derived from science has been dominant. The quiet growth of the natural sciences has coloured the whole mentality of the modern man. Even philosophy, which should be the architect of all the buildings of the Spirit, is tinged with the colouring of some imaginative background; this background is now supplied by natural science.

Science is not rationalistic in the sense in which the scholastic philosophy was rationalistic. Science begins with brute facts; rationalism tries to give reasons for all such facts. Nevertheless I cannot agree with Whitehead that the classical controversy between Galileo and the Church was one of anti-intellectualism (an objectionable word!) against the rationalism of orthodoxy. In the first place Whitehead has not mentioned the supernaturalistic dualism which dominated medieval thought, and which is, above all other theories, destructive of the very foundations of science. The dualism of natural and supernatural had, as I have said already, begun to take the place of the earlier dualism of the absolute and the relative law of nature, which has been distorted in modern times into the wholly disastrous absolute dualism of public and private ethics. In the second place, Whitehead even maintains that Galileo's way of stating the facts was in itself not more true than the formulation of the Inquisition! This startling paradox, whether we call it relativism or pragmatism, seems to me to cut at the root of the belief in absolute truth. How, on this showing, can we laugh at the monkey-trial at Dayton, Tennessee, and how can we condemn the bad faith and the lies of Hitler and Goebbels?

Descartes is no doubt largely responsible for another dualism, which has divided philosophic thought into an idealism which puts matter inside mind, and the naïve realism or materialism which puts mind inside matter. The success of mathematical physics in dealing with abstractions foisted

nto philosophy the task of accepting them
as ultimate facts.

The insoluble contradiction between the
materialistic mechanism of science and the
ineradicable sense of spiritual values—religious, moral, and aesthetic—became explicit in the nineteenth century. As Whitehead says, some of the deeper thinkers among
theologians and philosophers in that century were 'muddled thinkers'. Tennyson,
Matthew Arnold, and Clough all express a
characteristic sense of doubt and perplexity.
The romantic reaction was a protest on behalf of value; but the prestige of naturalism
was so great that the protest was timid and
almost apologetic.

In the nineteenth century, science, which
had never troubled itself about Hume's re-
futation of its principles, advanced from
strength to strength. Romanticism, which
had inspired the Oxford movement and the
revival of Catholicism, was dispersed over
many divergent interests as the century
went on. But the most striking change was
the rapid progress in technology, or applied
science, which changed all the conditions of
social life.

Aristotle's famous prediction, which he never expected to be realised, that if looms and shuttles could move themselves, 'we should have no more need of slaves', was being quickly fulfilled. Technological method was systematised, especially in Germany. Every branch of study became more and more professionalised, not to the advantage of this country, where the gifted and versatile amateur has been more prominent than the university professor. There is a danger that the failure of the tower of Babel may be repeated; the specialists cannot always understand each other.

Cracks soon began to appear in the solid structure of science. We had been told confidently that the ether is the fundamental postulate of physics. Thirty years later a book on physics appeared in which the fundamental postulate is not even mentioned in the index. The minute billiard ball, the atom, proved to be a sort of miniature solar system. Our pundits are still not agreed whether light is undulatory or corpuscular. One of them confessed that they use the former of these theories on three days of the week, the latter on the other three. Aston's isotopes complicated the list of atomic weights. Einstein's theory of relativity, the doctrine that time is a fourth dimension, and Planck's quantum theory, take the layman quite out of his depth. The advocates of organism or emergent evolution refuse to be confined by the law of the mechanicists. The general public had hardly accepted Darwin's doctrine of evolution before Lamarckism began to raise its head again, and we were told that natural selection only eliminates and cannot create.

If we accept the view that the resistance offered by religion to nineteenth-century naturalism was a reasonable though rather muddle-headed protest on behalf of recognising the realm of value as (so to speak) another dimension, with as good a right to a place in the scheme of reality as the quantitative aspects acknowledged too exclusively by science, we shall be able to do justice to the apparently obstinate refusal of theology to receive the well-attested results of scientific research, while admitting at the same time that the defenders of orthodoxy tried to hold a number of indefensible positions, from which they were driven in succession, till religion seemed to be in retreat along the whole line. Every new discovery in nature was proclaimed as a victory for science and a defeat for religion. The real controversy was not nearly so simple as this. A great deal of bad science was mixed up with religious dogma, imbedded in it like a fly in amber, or, to vary the metaphor, it had served as a support round which faith had twined itself, and from which it could be detached only with great difficulty, when it became clear that faith could stand without it. When the limitations of scientific abstraction were recognised, the legitimacy of the religious protest was more generously admitted, and the problem now was to understand the function of myth, symbol, and poetry in adjusting religious values to the historical process. Much has been done since the beginning of the present century to bring both sides within the scope of a comprehensive philosophy. Institutional religion will always lag behind the thought of the most enlightened thinkers, because it must cater for those who rely upon inherited tradition; but it would be a mistake to argue from the defeatism of many of our representatives, or from the increasing neglect of obsolescent fashions of worship, to a real decay of Christianity. The main danger is that the Church may be tempted to be false to its principles, in the hope of regaining its popularity. A Church that goes into politics always comes out badly smirched. Power is always abused; a dominant party is always in the wrong. The court-chaplains of King Demos may betray their trust no less than the obsequious servants of autocrats and oligarchs.

We may now consider the fortunes of humanism from another angle, as illustrated in our literature. The Renaissance was the rebirth of the individual. It was a joyous recovery of freedom, which we are now steadily losing, in spite of vigorous movements of revolt. Tennyson might boast, not without reason, that England is a land where, girt with friends or foes, a man may speak the thing he will. But there was less freedom in the nineteenth century than in the eighteenth, and there is much less in the twentieth than in the nineteenth. This is mainly due to the growth of nationalism, the deadliest foe of freedom, but partly also to the complexity of modern industrialism. Every rise in the standard of living restricts our independence by multiplying our wants. The fusion of social classes, which had formerly almost the rigidity of a caste system, has made the position of a large section of the population less secure, and so imposed new shackles upon liberty. Mass production turned the independent craftsman once more into Aristotle's 'animated tool'. His employer was equally the servant of a system from which he could not escape. Even newspapers and authors are far more dependent on a large and ill-educated public than they formerly were. In politics it is notorious that every politician is bound hand and foot to the party machine. Education, like everything else, is being standardised. This loss of freedom is of course total under the new dictatorships. 'Man is only free', according to Mussolini, 'in and through the State. The whole can only be the sovereign State, which tolerates no discussion and no control.' But the evil is rampant in democracies. The citizen of Main Street, U.S.A., must dress and talk and behave like his neighbours, or suffer for not doing so.

The generation after the Napoleonic War in some ways resembled the twenty years through which we have just passed. There were alternations of boom and slump, false dawns of prosperity, years of hardship for the poor like those which made the hungry 'forties a proverb, and a mixture of optimism and pessimism, in which pessimism predominated. The period ended in an outburst of prosperity such as the country had not seen before and will certainly not see again.

I have spoken of the intellectual difficulties of the Victorians. Carlyle, who had studied the great German idealists and Goethe, thought he had found bedrock beneath the quagmire. But there is something strained in *Sartor Resartus*. Carlyle is writing to convince himself. He is far from optimistic about the future of England. Newman, at a time when English thought was perhaps more isolated from the Continent than ever before or since, hoped to revive pre-Reformation Christianity, a hopeless dream of the new romanticism; but after a few years he lost heart, and gave up the hope of moving a society which seemed to him to be sunk in materialism and infidelity.

217

We are often surprised at the extreme
violence of our men of letters at this time.
On the Continent men were being flogged,
hanged and shot, while we muddled through
troubles without bloodshed. But we relieved
our minds by furious denunciation. Carlyle,
Hazlitt, Ruskin and others saw society in
silhouette, and the black portion of the picture covered nearly the whole space. These
diatribes were not modified after the turn of
the tide, when the hungry 'forties gave place
to the expansion of prosperity 'by leaps and
bounds'. Outraged romanticism perceived
that trade and commerce were now the
dominant interests in a society which was
very naturally eager to make the most of
unique opportunities. It is not quite clear
what Carlyle wished to substitute for what
he called the pig-philosophy of political economy. He appealed to the landed aristocracy, who had abdicated at the first Reform
Bill, to give up hunting foxes and shooting
partridges and lead the nation to more
worthy pursuits. But he had nothing but
contempt for the Catholic revival, and declared that Newman had less brains than a
rabbit. At a time when, as we look back

218

upon it, there was an astonishing vigour of individualism and originality, Emerson, Mill and Disraeli agree that 'individuality is dead'. Some of these critics, like the rhetorical and futile Russian 'intelligentsia' of a later generation, were more ready to shriek that the country was going to the dogs than to suggest practical remedies. Dickens won great popularity by exposing the abuses of the day before yesterday; Disraeli, in the golden age of the middle class, divided the country into rich and poor.

It is quite true that Mammon, 'the least exalted spirit that fell', was driving into the background man's interest in the higher values. The Victorian critics could not foresee that our abounding prosperity must soon come to an end, and that meanwhile it was inevitable that the most energetic and ambitious members of the community should wish to make hay while the sun shone. In their disgust with commercialism the critics of society at this time did not realise that it was doing much to purge Britain of the barbarous and disreputable vices which had brutalised the lower orders in the eighteenth century and the drunken and profligate

aristocracy of the Regency. Like most prophets they were a generation behind the
times in their jeremiads, just as our minor
prophets go on denouncing 'the sickness of
an acquisitive society' at a time when Mammon has very little to offer to his votaries,
and when a naturally indolent nation has
relapsed into pleasure-hunting and betting.
Contemporary thought is always out of
date.

Ruskin had a deeper vision than most of
his contemporaries. He saw clearly that
mechanisation was depriving labour of its
dignity and interest, and that the un-
paralleled ugliness of the modern town was
a symptom of spiritual disease. He looked at
the medieval cathedral, and thought of the
skilled craftsmen who, if not the architects,
were the executants of so much beauty. He
perhaps forgot that the majority of work-
men at that time were not carving angels or
gargoyles but quarrying stones or dragging
them uphill with their own muscles. But
his demand that the joy of creation must
somehow be restored to labour was true and
timely; it is a problem which has not yet
been solved, except for the small minority of

skilled mechanics, scholars, researchers, men
of letters, and artists. He also saw that industrialism was being corrupted; that the
small manufacturer was being superseded
by the soulless joint-stock company, and that
the largest fortunes were made not by producing useful commodities but by trading
in money. Grievous injury and insult were
offered to the workers by compelling them
to make things that nobody ought to want.
The 'economic man' is a figment, since economics are only one among many of the
interests of life, and 'the laws of supply and
demand' are no fixed laws, but depend on
what the consumer desires and is able to pay
for.

Ever since the Renaissance, the artistic
and literary ideal had been competing with
the positivist and scientific spirit, and now it
was plain that culture was losing the battle.
Ruskin, who like Wordsworth and many
other Englishmen was a Platonist, was willing to sacrifice some of our material prosperity if our countrymen could recover
their sense of the higher values. It may be
disputed whether he or William Morris did
most in this crusade, which was far from

being a complete failure. Like Plato himself, they were both in intention constructive, and like Plato they found that the building of an ideal Republic was beyond their powers. The influence of the prophet on practical politics is indirect and usually posthumous.

Matthew Arnold, a humanist of the purest water, who lived in the classical tradition, divides his fellow-countrymen into barbarians, Philistines, and populace. All three sections deserved their nicknames, though Arnold's manner was needlessly irritating. We have only to look at the library in an average rich man's house to see how far that class has degenerated from the scholarly tradition of the eighteenth century. The Philistines of suburbia are not interesting to talk to, though they are not so blatantly contemptuous of culture as Matthew Arnold's Mr. Bottles. There has been most improvement in the 'populace', who no longer love 'hustling, bawling, and smashing'. But the tastes of the populace, as revealed in their favourite newspapers, are still rather vile. Arnold in his later books is more interested in religion than in anything else.

222

He pins his faith on an Erasmian reformation in the Church of England, the prospects of which do not at present seem to be very favourable.

The mid-Victorian pictures of social life in the upper and middle classes, among which the novels of Anthony Trollope are now again the most popular, show that home life was healthier and happier than in the days when the head of the household spent his spare time at a club, or bullied his children like Mr. Fairchild, perhaps the most odious character in fiction. The home was a refuge where the economic man could forget his label; he could there escape from the arena of cut-throat competition and the prison of monotonous drudgery into the place where communism is really a success—the family. The middle-class wife was no longer so much enslaved by child-bearing and household cares; she had some leisure, and could cultivate her mind. The picture is on the whole a very agreeable one. The chief drawback is the ultra-romantic idea of love between the sexes, which vitiates the plots of many Victorian novels and makes them almost unreadable. The disintegration of

223

the home circle in the twentieth century
is one of the greatest evils of our time, even
when we remember how many daughter
in the middle class sacrificed their happines
to the supposed duty of taking care of ar
ageing and selfish parent. Samuel Butler'
The Way of all Flesh is a travesty. Old
people at Shrewsbury who knew the Butler
family were indignant at the misrepresen
tation of it by a man who, in spite of hi
brilliant gifts, was quite destitute of natura
affection.

In those sections of society where boys are
sent to boarding-schools from the ages of ten
to eighteen or nineteen, they do not see
much of their homes. These institutions
especially the public schools, have been sub
jected to a great deal of criticism. It is said
that they keep alive class distinctions which
are out of date, and which would otherwise
die a natural death. The great expense of a
'gentleman's education', which may cost a
boy's father three thousand pounds, has a
good deal to do with the undesirably low
birth-rate in the professional class. Economi
cally, it is a bad investment, for the young
artisan, who has been educated at the ex

pense of the taxpayer, and very largely at the expense of those who do not make use of the State schools, often earns, at the age of twenty-five, a larger income than the public school and university man. The education given at a public school is said to be chiefly directed to the formation of character, and of the kind of character which was formerly useful in a dominant and privileged class. Intellectually, the public school is said to be sterilising. The subjects taught, and the manner of teaching them, do not interest the majority of the boys, and in many schools public opinion discourages intellectual keenness. Lastly it is said that to segregate boys from the other sex and from older people leads to practices which are morally pernicious, and which if they are persisted in after schooldays often end in lamentable tragedies.

The financial ruin which must follow the present war will give a death-blow to most of the public schools and to the class which supports them. These institutions, in spite of their faults, awaken a love and loyalty in their old members which are quite peculiar to this country, and which will save some of

them, at least for a time, from the fate
which seems to be inevitable. This affection
is a fact which should not be forgotten by
those who can see only the evils and ana-
chronisms of the system. These evils are not
so rampant as they were fifty years ago. The
curriculum is more varied and more rational.
The absurd worship of athletic prowess is
curbed in some public schools, though not in
all. When a boy goes to the university, he no
longer associates only with his parents' class,
for a large proportion of undergraduates are
now State-aided students from board-schools.
As for the morals of the boys, schoolmasters
well understand the need for supervision,
and the schoolboy is free from some temptations of the same kind which might assail him
if he were at home.

Still, it is a significant fact that after
Matthew Arnold and Pater very few great
literary reputations have been made by men
who have been educated in the classical
tradition, and even among the earlier
generation the most famous names, such as
Tennyson, Browning, Ruskin, Dickens, and
Mill are not on the roll of any great school.
Talent, says Goethe, is formed in isolation,

character in the stream of the world. The budding genius is refractory to the discipline of public opinion at a large school. He is often bullied and unhappy; and we cannot tell how many who might otherwise have won high distinction have been cramped and discouraged by that unsympathetic atmosphere.

In the last twenty years of the nineteenth century the arrogance and ambition of Great Britain reached its climax. It was not cruel or brutal, though it was frequently grossly insulting to other nations, as we may see from some amazing cartoons in *Punch*. Its most brilliant prophet, Rudyard Kipling, though he permitted himself to speak of 'lesser breeds without the law,' i.e. foreigners in general, was sincerely anxious that his countrymen should take up the white man's burden in a serious spirit of devotion to duty; and when the old century gave place to the new he became thoroughly alarmed at the black clouds which he saw gathering on the horizon, and at the fatuous frivolity which refused to see that all was not well. 'Let him that thinketh he standeth take heed lest he fall;' or as the Latin poet Publilius Syrus puts it, '*Ubi nil timetur, quod timeatur nascitur.*'

The 'nineties were not specially 'naughty'. Decadent aestheticism was superficial and shortlived. There was a great deal of almost first-rate talent among unbalanced romantics, most of whom died young, with or without the assistance of drugs. But it was an age of roaring bumptiousness, which ought not to be confused with the complacency of the earlier Victorian age, any more than the living-rooms of the period, choked with unnecessary furniture and so-called ornaments, were characteristic of the dignified and even beautiful rooms of a hundred years ago. An Old Testament prophet or a Greek tragedian, noting the plethoric exuberance of John Bull, would have prophesied disaster with even more emphasis than Kipling's 'Lest we forget'.

The isolation of the British tradition in literature had now come to an end. Our novelists and dramatists had studied French, Scandinavian, and Russian models. It was a dangerous experiment. We are safest when we are content to be ourselves. The French, the most civilised nation in Europe, can per-

haps rely on their fundamental sanity so far
as to dispense with inhibitions which we have
instinctively regarded as necessary to healthy-
mindedness. The Italians long ago said that
an Italianised Englishman is an incarnate
devil. French romanticism, when it is lived
as well as preached, is often poisonous. If
we compare Tennyson with de Musset or
Baudelaire, George Eliot with George Sand,
or Meredith with Flaubert, we shall find in
some of the Frenchmen a positive cult of
morbidity, almost proud of its departure
from traditional ideas of healthiness. As a
pendant to diseased romanticism we have the
stark realism of Zola, which is somehow
much more unclean in English than in
French, and the tedious adultery-motif which
has given the world an unfair opinion of
domestic life in France. In art the Quartier
Latin has broken out in sheer insanity, the
Fauves, the Dadaists, and similar groups.
Our own art critics have intimidated the
public into pretending to admire exotic rub-
bish of this kind. Nor has the influence of
Ibsen been altogether beneficial. After all,
he depicts the most provincial manners of a
small country. In Russian literature there is

229

a strange unfamiliar attraction. Men and women seem to act from motives unintelligible to us in the West.

Queen Victoria's death was really the end of an age, if any date can be assigned to changes which never come suddenly. It coincided with the end of the imperialist dream, which, though not base, was quite out of touch with reality. The humiliations of the Boer War were salutary; they pricked the bubble of our inflated self-esteem, and revealed the failure of what was then a privileged class to make politics and administration efficient. The outburst of hatred of England on the Continent in those years was not very unlike our indignation to-day at the aggression of strong nations upon weak; but it was also a sign of the growing jealousy of fevered nationalism at the spectacle of a nation which had played the game of grab too successfully. We thought it unjust, as it was; we despised it, which was not wise.

The Edwardian age was terminated not by the beginning of a new reign but by the outbreak of the Great War. It is usual now to describe it as a time of reckless licence and self-indulgence. This, I think, is wisdom after the event. Some of our politicians, no doubt, realised the gravity of the German menace, and after vain efforts, frustrated mainly by the sinister Holstein, to come to a friendly understanding with Germany, they secured for Japan a free hand in trying conclusions with Russia at the expense of Corea, concluded an entente with France at the expense of Morocco, and with Russia at the expense of Persia. These, it seemed, were not nations rightly struggling to be free. But the mass of Englishmen, as far as my recollection goes, never thought of war as a certainty or even as a probability, nor had they any acute consciousness that their country was at the end of a golden age.

The chief characteristic of these thirteen years was the extreme violence of sectional animosities, the very opposite of the concentrated nationalism which was to crush all such movements on the Continent after the war. Party politics were pursued with reckless bitterness. The two Houses of Parliament threatened a constitutional crisis of the first magnitude. Ireland was almost in a state of civil war. Labour agitation, now thoroughly organised, promoted strikes

231

aimed not at the employers but at the entire community. The war came only just in time to forestall a revolutionary strike which was fixed for the autumn of 1914. Gangs of female hooligans, who professed to be agitating for the parliamentary vote, committed criminal and senseless outrages. Such a state of things struck at the roots of popular government, and made the Germans think that they were attacking a decadent nation.

The main cause of these outbreaks was probably one which has not received sufficient attention, namely boredom. No nation can stand being rationally and pacifically governed for more than a few years. Rational politics are dull; patriotism languishes for want of any obvious enemy. This strange perversity of human nature would soon break up a farmyard of tame Fabian socialists, as it broke up the comfortable bourgeois monarchy of Louis Philippe.

The devil of fissiparous sectionalism was driven out by Beelzebub the chief of the devils. Unrestricted nationalism brought about the Great War, and the danger, not of defeat but of destruction, submerged for a time the anti-social intransigences of the Edwardian period. The war, and still more the peace, showed that the principle of nationalism had won. The League of Nations was, as Christopher Dawson has said, a crystallisation of the European State-system at the moment when it was most completely disintegrated by national particularism. The war began in the Balkans, and ended in the Balkanisation of Europe. In the past, State, nation, and civilisation were three separate things; now there was to be no higher unity than the State.

To turn to domestic politics. Without humanism, or rather humanitarianism, the victory of democracy would not have been possible. But since political democracy did not lead to economic equality, the disappointed classes were attracted by State socialism, which is the negation of liberty and potentially the ally of militarism, since a nation in arms must organise itself in this way. For socialism, though in its origin it may deserve to be called 'individualism run mad', ends by suppressing the individual and almost denying him the right to exist as an individual. This is what has happened in all

233

the totalitarian States, and with the rights of the individual has disappeared the humanitarianism which was the first mainspring of the whole movement. In the democratic countries there has so far been no recrudescence of cruelty, but over the greater part of Europe the most shocking outrages against individuals, classes, and nations are accepted as part of the order of things. The loss of liberty has also dried up the sources of intellectual activity. The countrymen of Goethe, of Leonardo, and of Tolstoi no longer make any valuable contribution to the culture of the world. 'The government of the world', says Bertrand Russell, 'has been allowed to fall into the hands of men ignorant of the past, without tenderness to what is traditional, without understanding of what they are destroying. The new society is incompatible with the pursuit of truth, with love, with art, with spontaneous delight, with every ideal that men have cherished, with the sole exception of ascetic renunciation.'

The average man, at least in this country, has not given up the ideas of humanism or humanitarianism. In a new *Anthology of Prayer*, edited by Muriel Box, there is a typical modern prayer, which I think expresses the week-day religion of the average Englishman well enough.

Give me a good digestion, Lord,
And also something to digest;
Give me a healthy body, Lord,
With sense to keep it at its best.

Give me a healthy mind, O Lord,
To keep the good and pure in sight,
Which seeing sin is not appalled,
But finds a way to set it right.

Give me a mind that is not bored,
That does not whimper, whine, or sigh;
Don't let me worry overmuch
About the fussy thing called I.

Give me a sense of humour, Lord,
Give me the grace to see a joke,
To get some happiness from life
And pass it on to other folk.

This pleasant creed falls short of human needs at their best. Man is a queer animal, for he is capable of martyrdom. It is not enough to supply all his material wants. He needs an ideal to live for, an ideal for which if necessary he is willing to die. This means that there are absolute values, and that neither life nor pleasure is one of them. There is a world of eternal spiritual realities in which and for which we are living. When this is once admitted, all political and economic values are seen to be only relative and subsidiary. In thus taking their proper place, they cease to be legitimate causes of internecine strife. Science obviously cannot take the place of the absolute values, being an abstract study, limited to quantitative aspects of reality; but truth, to which the scientist devotes his life, is an absolute value, as even the agnostic may be constrained to admit if we ask him why he prefers truth to error.

This recognition of objective values is part of the humanist tradition as it comes down from Plato. When we speak of the failure of humanism we do not mean, or ought not to mean, that the ideal of humanism is wrong, even if we believe that it needs to be supplemented by the Christian law of love. It has failed, as Christianity may be said to have failed, because in our generation men have forgotten it or do not try to live up to it. The young, says Professor Joad in a recent

236

book, wander aimlessly along the road of
life without knowing whither they are
travelling, or why they travel at all. They are
without creed or code, standards or values.
To all intents and purposes they are without
religious belief. There is a general repudiation of all restraints and inhibitions. They
have learned from the psycho-analysts that
the suppression of instinct and the thwarting
of desire are harmful. The lives of many of
them are shadowed by the fear of war and of
unemployment. 'Everything is frightful,'
they say to one another. 'Let us go and have
a drink and then dance.' There is a positive
snobbery of anti-culture. They do not read
the literature even of their own age. A life
without standards or values is necessarily
bored and boring, and the young generation
are bored.

This is the experience of a man who sees
much of the young. The picture may be, and
I think is, painted in too dark colours; the
Professor's young friends seem to be chiefly
disgruntled ex-Communists. But it is too
plain that those who would perhaps call
themselves humanists have, for the most
part, no clearly envisaged standards of value.

Their creed might be summed up in the lines of the Australian poet Lindsay Gordon:

> *'Life is mainly froth and bubble ;*
> *Two things stand like stone ;*
> *Kindness in another's trouble,*
> *Courage in your own.'*

It may seem far-fetched to look for guidance to Athens in the fourth century before Christ. But the troubles of Greece in the age of Plato were very much like those which surround us to-day.

The habit of critical and scientific thought was the great gift of Greece. But it brought an intellectual upheaval which combined with the shock of a great war to unsettle the minds of the people. The so-called Sophists, professional teachers and lecturers, raised the fundamental question whether the moral law was only convention, or whether it had an independent sanctity. This was to cut at the root of all accepted standards of right and wrong. Some of them taught, like Nietzsche, that justice and mercy are the inventions of the many to protect themselves against the few, who being superior beings ought to rule. Plato, in the *Laws*, shows how the

materialist of his time repudiated all teleo-
ogy and all rationality in nature. 'The gods
have no existence; they are the creation of
rt and convention. Nor is there any such
hing as natural right; mankind are always
ltering rights, and every change is valid.
Right is whatever a man can carry with the
high hand. Hence our epidemics of youthful
rreligion.' The Greeks were more radical
and ruthless than most of our writers; but
such a description as Plato's does not sound
unfamiliar. Nor is there anything strange to
us in the words of Critias that 'some clever
men invented the fear of God, so that there
might be something of which men were
afraid, even in their secret deeds and words
and thoughts, a Being who would hear all
that men said and see all their actions, and
even their unspoken plans for sin.' That religion is the joint product of the duplicity of
the first knave and the simplicity of the first
fool is an opinion common in rationalist
societies and elsewhere.

The threatened break-up of all traditional
morality was arrested, in no small measure,
by Plato himself, or, as he would have said,
by his master Socrates. He puts the question

fairly and squarely. Are there such things as
objective values, which stand in their own
right, and are not the product of men or
societies? Are justice and truth and the love
of the beautiful natural to man? He answers,
in the *Republic*, 'Goodness is the health and
beauty and well-being of the soul; evil is its
disease, deformity, and weakness.' What
really satisfies man? We must examine
human nature carefully to find the answer;
the unexamined life is not worth living. The
spirit of man, when properly trained, can
give a clear answer; the fully real can be fully
known. The philosophy which can be so
summed up is able to give civilisation a soul,
and men and women a principle to live by.
The Platonic Socrates would have made
short work of the inane catchwords which
do duty for thought among our contemporaries.

It is of course most unfair to compare the
wisest of the Greeks with the modern man
in the street. The Greeks were not all Platos;
they disliked Socrates so much that they
condemned him to death. The Athenians, at
the height of their power and glory, deliberately ordered the massacre of the whole

male population of Melos—'and many other
such-like things they did.' My only point is
that at a time of crisis not unlike that in
which we are living they, through their
most influential teachers, found a way out by
firmly asserting the objectivity of the absolute values against the disintegrating relativism and scepticism of the age, and by
doing so gave Hellenism a long lease of
beneficent life. For Platonism, in its fundamental principles, never died. In its Christianised form it still lives, and needs only
to be accepted as the faith of the nation for
most of our social maladies to be cured.

If we could visit ancient Greece in the
fourth century before Christ, we should be
amazed at the simplicity and poverty of the
country, and especially by the contrast between the keen intellectual interests of a
populace which could flock to hear a trilogy
by Aeschylus or Sophocles as our countrymen flock to what they call the pictures, and
the extreme backwardness of the Greeks in
technology. It is not enough to recall some
undoubtedly snobbish disparagements of
honest labour, nor the fact that slave-labour
always discourages invention. Both Plato and

Aristotle distrusted and disliked any changes
of habit which made life more complicated.
Plato was disgusted with the self-indulgence
of the Sicilians, who actually took two heavy
meals every day. And Aristotle in a very
instructive passage says that 'while at first
it was natural that anyone who invented an
art that went beyond the common percep-
tions of men should be admired, not merely
for any utility in his discovery, but because
he was regarded as wise and superior to his
fellows; with the progress of technical inventions, some bearing on the necessities of life
and others on rational enjoyment, we have
come to regard the inventions of the latter
as wiser than those of the former, because
they do not aim at utility.' The contrast between this standard of values and that which
until very lately prevailed in Europe and in
the United States, is brought out amusingly in
Mr. Woodroffe's skit, *Plato's American Republic*. I think it is plain that Christ believed
that the conditions to which he was accustomed in His Galilean home—the very simple
life of a hardy and industrious peasantry—
are the most favourable for the spiritual life.
'Worldly cares', which increase with every

rise in the standard of living, 'choke the word and make it unfruitful.' This is the exact contrary of the ideal of 'consumptionism', which should not be called humanistic. I have elsewhere called attention to the extraordinary longevity of the Greeks in their golden age. They were eminently healthy as well as beautiful.

But the most precious legacy of Greek philosophy is the firm belief in absolute values. This is a point which is often confused. The question, 'What is my duty?' often requires careful consideration, and our decision must be relative to the circumstances. But the question, 'If I know my duty, why should I do it?' admits of no answer except 'Because it is your duty.' We are here in contact with an ultimate, which in this case speaks in the imperative mood. In the same way, we may be doubtful what is the truth, but if we know it we cannot prefer falsehood without treason to one of the attributes under which God has revealed Himself to us.

We recall the unforgettable passage in Plato's *Republic* in which Adeimantus draws two pictures—one of a consummate scoundrel who after a successful career dies in the odour of sanctity, and the other of a perfectly righteous man who after being calumniated and persecuted is at last tortured and —crucified. Which of these two lives, he asks, would anyone choose? It is a question which bites deeply, but only one answer is possible. 'If a man desires the good life for any reason outside itself,' says Plotinus, 'it is not the good life that he desires.'

Psychology cannot alter this decision by making morality subjective and relative. If psychology is merely the study of human behaviour, it belongs to the natural sciences, and like all the natural sciences is abstract and incomplete. But if, with the Platonists, we mean by psychology the metaphysics of the human mind, we shall treat it with much more respect. For according to this school the soul is the wanderer in the realm of reality, having affinities with planes of being both above and below itself. When 'the soul becomes spirit' it has its home in the eternal world, and apprehends the ultimate values, not as unrealised ideals, but as objective realities. Their authority over us is absolute.

All this is humanism at its best, and it

would be ours even without the Christian revelation. What then is the contribution of Christianity; for it is admitted that under the Roman empire there was a fusion of these two rivers, the Hellenic and the Jewish?

Judaism, the religion of southern Palestine, did not contribute much. It rejected the new revelation, and crucified its Prophet. From that time to this, Christianity has been the least Asiatic, the least Semitic, of the great religions. The Semites either retained their old religion or accepted Islam, which Westcott called petrified Judaism. In this creed the divine omnipotence blazes in hard and solitary splendour, like the sun over the desert.

Perhaps the chief contribution of Judaism was the desire and expectation that God's justice may be established on earth. Even Plato says, 'Human affairs are not worth serious attention. The worst of it is that we are obliged to take them seriously.' Plotinus, Spinoza, and many of the mystics answer, 'But why then should we take them seriously?' Spinoza was a Jew, but this way of thinking has never been characteristic of his nation.

But the greatest contribution of Christianity to Hellenistic religion is one which comes from the Founder Himself rather than from His nation—the law of love. The Platonists realised that love is the chief hierophant of the divine mysteries; the spirit in love sees the beatific vision. But love to man, as the sacrament and necessary manifestation of love to God—this doctrine, so closely connected with the Incarnation, gives warmth, fire, and colour to the somewhat cold 'scale of perfection' mapped out for us by the Greek philosophers. It sweeps away that last infirmity of noble minds, the wish to be invulnerable, the promise of other religions and philosophies; for love often hurts. Remembering this, we may say that humanism is 'not enough'. But let us not disparage it; it may make us civilised, which most of us are not at present.

VI
RELIGION

VI

RELIGION

The question was often asked during the Great War whether it would make the people of this country more or less religious. The wisest answer was that it would stimulate the lower kind of religion and depress the higher. Faith in the providential ordering of the world was severely shaken by the outbreak of a fierce war between Christian nations. The atrocities committed by the Germans, which lost nothing in the telling, seemed to prove not only that Christian Europe was making no progress in humanity, but that the forces of evil were stronger than the forces of good. The exacerbation of national hatred, which is part of the technique of modern war, is itself a repudiation of the religion of love. On the other hand, superstitions of every kind, which in normal times are driven underground or half-accepted in humorous make-believe, recovered their credibility. In particular, necromancy, which had long been exploited by fraud and

credulity without making many real converts, found ready listeners among those
who had suffered bereavement in the war.

Besides this, the crisis acted in favour of
pragmatism. Intellectual judgments on traditional beliefs were thrust aside with impatience. People could not afford, in such
hard times, to dispense with any comforting
assurances. The tide of irrationalism in
philosophy had been rising for some years
before the war. Traditionalists began to
congratulate themselves that Liberal theology was on the wane. The young were not
attracted by it. Hitler has expressed his admiration of the tactics of the Roman Catholic Church, which refuses to retract anything,
and insists on unquestioning submission to
orthodox dogmas as a whole. This is the
method of every totalitarian State.

It is true that Modernism in that Church
seems to have been effectually silenced, and
if it had had much force behind it, it could
hardly have been suppressed so easily. But
the attack on miracles is no longer a matter
of great interest in the Roman communion,
where the revival of the Thomist philosophy
in the hands of several very able exponents

has given a new impetus to the study of the philosophy of religion. The Roman apologists now hold the foremost place as defenders of what they call the *philosophia perennis*—Christianised Platonism and Aristotelianism—against the new philosophies which compete with each other for the allegiance of the young. As much of the new philosophy is anti-intellectual, the Liberal theologian, in spite of his dislike of supernaturalistic dualism, finds himself in more sympathy with the Catholic controversialists than with their opponents.

I wish to consider the present state and future prospects of Christianity in this country from the point of view of one who believes in the *philosophia perennis*, or, as I should say, Christianised Platonism, in opposition to the disintegrating relativism of much recent thought. Believing as I do in intellectual honesty, and in the authority of science within its own field, I am strongly opposed to what the Americans call fundamentalism, and to what seems to me the reactionary or obscurantist theology of Karl Barth in Germany.

Nor can I agree with the supreme position

251

given to history by the Italian New Idealists
and others. History can establish truths only
on its own plane. Religious truth is super-
historical. Facts of history are not objects of
religious faith, though they may have a
sacramental value for those who believe in
divine revelation. The mind of God does not
change, nor can any events in time alter the
laws which the Creator has laid down for
His creatures. But eternal truth must be revealed to man under the conditions of his
present life; and as the conditions are not
always equally favourable, revelation must
be imparted 'at sundry times and in divers
manners'. Ideas, it has been said, must be
given through something, and religious revelation has not been able to dispense with
symbol, myth, and poetry. Even philosophy,
if it aspires to be what it used to be called,
the *ars vitae*, must contain an element of
myth. Of this Plato was well aware. His
myths are concerned with eschatology, i.e.
with regions where science and reason must
acknowledge their limitations.

It is no disparagement to the reason to
own that there are limits to the knowledge
which it can give us. Goethe says: 'Man's

252

highest happiness as a thinker is to have
fathomed what can be fathomed, and to bow
in reverence before the unfathomable.' As
Meyerson has shown in his famous book on
the philosophy of science, we must accept
certain brute facts and values of which no
explanation can be given. We do not know
why the world exists. We cannot say that
space and time are infinite, nor that they are
not infinite. Both hypotheses land us in
riddles which we cannot solve. We may
compare, if we will, the realm of values to
another dimension, not less real than space
and time, but not to be brought under those
categories. And within the realm of values
we may distinguish some which are relative
and instrumental from others which seem to
be absolute. It is usual to acknowledge three
absolute values, Truth, Goodness, and
Beauty. These exist in their own right. They
are not means to anything outside themselves, nor to each other. They are a three-
fold cord, not quickly broken. They are so
interwoven that if any one of them is discarded the other two are mutilated and lose
their absolute quality. But it is not correct to
say that 'Beauty is Truth, Truth Beauty,'

nor to confine Truth to the conclusion of a
syllogism or to the findings of natural
science. Nor is it correct to interpret the
universe in a purely moralistic manner. God
manifests Himself in other ways.

There are limits to human reason, and
human reason can discern and acknowledge
these limits. This we could not do, if there
were not in us a faculty superior to the discursive reason, which can use this reason as
its instrument. This faculty the Greeks
called *Nous,* a word for which we have no
equivalent. The words 'intellect, intelligence, reason' are all misleading, and have
misled many thinkers who have accused
Greek thought, and especially Plato and
Aristotle, of what they call intellectualism.
The same charge has been brought against
their Christian followers in the middle ages,
such as Thomas Aquinas. The charge of
intellectualism (a word with which we could
well dispense) is not justified against Platonism; Professor Burnet has rebutted this
charge conclusively and with indignation. A
too confident use of logic, which may fail us
when we are using terms which have no
fixed or definite connotation, is perhaps a

defect of scholasticism, though we can hardly pass from St. Thomas to many modern philosophers without regretting the loss of the clear-cut logical reasoning which distinguishes the great schoolmen.

I have myself used the word 'Spirit' as the least misleading equivalent of *Nous*. So Arnou has used *Esprit*, and German writers *Geist*. Lossky in the English translation of his works has used 'Spirit'. St. Paul's *Pneuma* is really the same, and some of the Greek Fathers recognise *Pneuma* as the Christian form of *Nous*. The Greek word for the discursive reason is *Dianoia*, which is kept in its proper place by Aristotle. Spinoza distinguishes between *ratio* and *scientia intuitiva*; Coleridge and Wordsworth between 'understanding' and 'reason', using the latter word for the scholastic *intellectus*. This use of 'reason' for the higher faculty was probably due to Coleridge, who had studied the Germans. In post-Kantian idealism the two faculties, instead of being confused, are sometimes too sharply separated, a serious error which involves what has been called the faculty-psychology, as if the human mind were not a unity. *Nous* is not exactly a faculty, but the whole personality acting under the guidance of its highest part, which like the Pauline *Pneuma* is superhuman and superpersonal. The separation of 'reason' and 'understanding' has been pushed so far in some recent philosophy as to disparage logic and intellect, and to make religion 'irrational', a word of which some German thinkers are not afraid. This contempt for reasoning, which is surely not far from blasphemy against the Holy Spirit, who was invoked as the giver of 'wisdom and understanding, of counsel and might, of knowledge and the fear of the Lord' at the General Councils of the Church, has had a disastrous effect on the minds of the present generation, far beyond the direct influence of professional philosophers. It is carried to an extreme in the works of William James, whom even Whitehead regards as a great philosopher. Faith, as Professor de Burgh says, is at least as fallible as logic, and 'wishful thinking' is a snare to everybody.

If we may accept our comparison of the realm of value to another dimension, the difficulty of correlating it with other dimensions is very great. We cannot acquiesce in an ultimate or irreconcilable dualism of fact and value. A fact which has no value is not a fact; a value which is not a fact is not a value. The statement, often made, that science deals with facts in abstraction from values is not correct, for science is wholly devoted to the service of truth, which is one of the ultimate values. But science does neglect, as unmanageable for its own purposes, those values which cannot be measured, weighed, or counted, and this restriction of scope makes it impossible to base a philosophy on natural science only. Philosophy takes all reality for its province, and our affirmations of value are as much worthy of respect as the verdicts of our senses. In the same way, religion can exclude no aspect of reality, though being essentially concerned with the higher values it arranges experience hierarchically, assigning a higher degree both of value and of reality to those aspects of experience in which the Spirit 'bears witness with our spirit' that we are in touch with a sphere above that in which we commonly live. The problem is how to bring these higher visions into connexion with the world of claims and counter-claims in which our lot is cast.

I recall with satisfaction a speech which I once made as the guest of the Worshipful Company of Spectacle-makers, in which I said that the clergy and other religious teachers are spectacle-makers. It is our business to provide spectacles to help people to see the invisible. It is a very difficult profession; for not only do men and women need a good deal of training before they can see the invisible, but no two people need exactly the same spectacles, nor does any person need the same pair when he is old that he did when he was young.

Another simile might compare the function of religious symbols to that of a bridge, which connects the realm of facts with the realm of values, or, which is much the same thing, the things which are seen and are temporal with the things which are not seen and are eternal. A bridge is of no use unless it touches both banks. We may add that there are many people who do not need the bridge because they do not wish to cross. There are a few, the contemplative mystics, who live on the further shore, 'prayer all their business, all their pleasure praise.' Types and figures do not interest them; they

258

have their footing in the 'intelligible world', 'yonder', and will let this world go hang. On the other side there is a much larger number who do not wish to cross because they are content with the world of sense. If they have any interest in religion, they materialise the poetry of religion and turn it into a series of flat historical recitals. Supernaturalism is the mysticism of the materialist.

To return to my spectacle-makers, we cannot have a stereotyped orthodoxy to suit both the learned professor and his kitchen-maid, and even in a world dominated by the inverted snobbery of democratism we cannot allow the great army of kitchen-maids to call the tune. It is pathetic, but not respectable, to see a learned man protesting that from the highest point of view his education has been worse than useless, since it is a positive handicap for understanding divine truth.

Christianity, as I have said already, has never been a 'proletarian' [1] creed. It had its

---

[1] I cannot help regretting that that prodigious monument of learning, Professor Arnold Toynbee's *A Study of History*, has been to some extent marred by his use, in every chapter, of the objectionable word 'proletariat'. He may explain, as he does, that he uses it in a sense of

birth in Galilee, among a well-educated and independent peasantry—farmers, fishermen, and small tradesmen, like the family of the Founder Himself. In passing, as it did, within a few years of the Crucifixion, into the main current of Hellenistic civilisation, it made most of its converts in the lower middle class of the towns, including the domestic servants of the rich, who certainly did not live in *ergastula*. The Epistles of St. Paul and the other books of the New Testament were not written for uneducated readers. Pliny in Bithynia, while Trajan was emperor, found that there were Christians in every class of society. There is no slur upon Christianity in supposing that it arose among 'the submerged tenth'; but historically it happens to be quite untrue.

his own; but we cannot with impunity play tricks with words which have a very clear and generally accepted meaning. In this case, the meaning of 'proletariat' has been fixed by Marx; it means the oppressed manual workers, the so-called wage-slaves, as distinguished from the aristocracy and the bourgeoisie. The word has never had any appropriateness in the western democracies, which are more and more taking the form of great middle-class societies. There are no 'proletarians' in England, France, or the United States. Nor is it easy to recognise another favourite phrase of the author, 'the Dominant Minority', in our class of unrepresented taxpayers.

There has been an immense amount of research into Christian origins. As regards the Epistles of St. Paul the result of criticism has been on the whole conservative, though some scholars think that there have been interpolations. The Pastoral Epistles, in their present form, are probably not by the hand of the apostle, and those who read the Epistle to the Ephesians in the original find enough peculiarities in the style, though not in the matter, to make the authorship doubtful. Roman Catholic theologians still refer to the Epistle to the Hebrews as Pauline, but this is quite impossible. The other Epistles attributed to St. Paul are generally accepted as genuine, and they are our earliest Christian documents. Criticism of the four Gospels has not led to any certain results, though few scholars would now dispute that the Fourth Gospel was written by an unknown mystical theologian in Asia Minor between 95 and 125 A.D. It is an interpretation of the eternal significance of the Incarnation, rather than a report of discourses actually delivered by Christ when on earth. But the Synoptic problem is not only unsolved but insoluble. When a historical Person has been made the central figure of a religious cult, he is invested with all the qualities which his disciples consider to belong to such a Being. The society treasures, and perhaps amplifies, those of his recorded utterances which it finds helpful in catechising, in liturgical worship, and in controversy. We cannot be sure that other ages might not have made a somewhat different selection. We can also trace, all through the New Testament and in the early centuries of Church history, a progressive application of honorific attributes, the tribute of the faith and love of the Church, to 'the Lord', the *Kyrios Christos*, who was all, and more than all, that the Hellenistic mystery religions found in their cult-heroes.

Those who have studied the literature of the Synoptic problem, and other works on the origins and early growth of Christianity, are often left with a very painful feeling of uncertainty, precisely in that region where they most desire unassailable evidence. They may feel, as I do myself, and as many impartial scholars have testified with deep conviction, that both the character of Christ and most of his sayings have a distinctive character which stamps them as historical. But this is a subjective judgment, which does not convince everybody. Is our religion founded on a rock, or on shifting sand? Is it legitimate to call upon faith to give us unshakeable belief in events which are historically doubtful? This, I think, is the question which now drives perhaps the majority of thoughtful young people into reluctant agnosticism.

In the last century most Catholics submitted themselves, as they still do, to the authority of the Church, most Protestants to the authority of the Bible, which they believed to be verbally inspired. The collapse of this latter belief has driven some who desire the refuge of authority to accept that of the Roman Catholic Church. But what Lippmann calls the acids of modernity have eaten deeply into the deposit of tradition. We cannot, if we would, identify ourselves with medieval modes of thought; and to give unquestioning obedience to one among many authorities, though it may bring great peace of mind, is too much like believing because we choose, not a very dignified attitude for a rational being. I am therefore addressing myself to those for whom this way of escape is barred by their wish to play no tricks with their intellectual conscience.

However much, or however little, we may set down to the enthusiastic loyalty of the little flock of disciples in their records of the Saviour's life, it is historically certain that a spiritual illumination of unique purity and intensity took place in Palestine in the reign of Tiberius. It takes two to tell the truth, one to speak and one to hear; the soil must be ready as well as the seed. The quality of the revelation is there for all to see in the New Testament; if anyone doubts that here are 'the words of eternal life', we have no more to say to him.

In Palestine, where the revelation was first made, the seed fell on stony ground. If it had not spread, through the Jewish Diaspora, to the Graeco-Roman world, the Gospel might, humanly speaking, have petered out as an obscure Jewish sect, a little Khalifate in the family of the Founder. This however is not a unique example of a very strange pheno-menon. As the Jerusalem priesthood was too strong for the Christian mission, so the Brahmanic priesthood almost drove Buddh-ism out of India, to take firm root in China,

Burmah, and other countries. As, outside the religious sphere, Greece may be said to have died in giving birth to Hellenism, so the framework of the Roman Empire died in giving birth to the Catholic Church.

On alien soil the new religion had to compete with other mystery-religions, such as Orphism and the cults of Osiris and Mithra. That Christianity had more to offer than any of its rivals will hardly be disputed. But the same cause which put it at a disadvantage in Palestine favoured it in Pagan societies. Although, as I have said, there was much truth and spiritual beauty in some of the mysteries, and although the philosophy of religion has never reached greater heights of wisdom and insight than in the later school of Plato, the attempt to preserve continuity with the classical civilisation entangled Pagan reform movements with beliefs and practices which were not acceptable to the cosmopolitan crowd with which slavery and trade had filled the Roman empire. Impure rites, magic and astrology, as well as sacrifice to the 'genius' of the emperor, were hindrances which could not be shaken off within Paganism. The genuine Greeks and Romans

were almost extinct, and their place was being taken by a populace which had small
reason to revere their institutions, and which
was insensitive to their science, art, and
literature. The Church, however, was not
uncompromising; it carried off into its hive
most of the honey which was worth preserving, and which, but for it, must have
perished in the welter of barbarism which
nearly overwhelmed civilisation in the third
century, and completed its ruin in the fifth
and sixth.

The fixation of doctrine took place in a
tired and listless age, an age, moreover, when
the scientific temper was almost dead. We
are right to bear this in mind when in
studying early Christianity we are troubled
by the want of interest in social questions,
the absence of any hope of happier conditions on earth, the tendency to take flight
from the world in hermitages and ascetic
communities, the disproportionate emphasis
on sexual continence, and the readiness to
believe in miracles. These developments,
which have a ready explanation in the circumstances of a time of troubles, have permanently affected the attitude of the Cath-

olic Church towards ethics, politics, and natural science. In the unreformed Churches it will be difficult for institutional Christianity to get free from them, although they are not a necessary or legitimate outcome of the original Gospel.

At the time when the scientific view of the world returned to Europe, and returned with such vigour as to revolutionise men's view of reality, Christians were too busy cutting each other's throats to have leisure to attend to the deeper religious crisis. Both sides were hardened and coarsened by the struggle; both were driven to rely on crude external sanctions instead of spiritual conviction.

So the Church, which in the thirteenth century as in the fourth had been abreast of the secular enlightenment of the age, was left in an intellectual backwater, from which it has not yet emerged.

In part this backwardness is the inevitable nemesis of institutionalism. There is never much of a crowd at the narrow gate, and some of those who reach it can find their way in without guides. But a great Church needs the support of numbers; a great

Church aims at power. It must therefore win the adherence of the half-educated, and still worse of the half-converted. It must present itself in the form of crude superstition, and offer tremendous sanctions by gaudy and lurid pictures of future bliss and torment. This is the vulgar Christianity which is very commonly identified with the religion of Christ. Now that these dogmatic picture-books seem to be out of relation to the world we live in, and that these violent bribes and threats no longer attract or terrify us, it is often assumed that Christianity is dead or dying.

These disputable doctrines, it will be observed, refer to the past or the future. But religion belongs essentially to the eternal and the present. When we translate eternity into temporal succession, and the indwelling Spirit of God into a Power intervening occasionally to show its superiority to the laws of nature, we are making an accommodation to older habits of thought which we have really outgrown. We are not morally obliged to give our assent to statements which rest upon bad science and bad philosophy.

It is of course true that at the beginning of our era men were willing to accept suspensions of the ordinary course of nature without great surprise. Where there is no law there is no miracle. In educated circles at Rome at the end of the Republic it was not so; but even among these, portents were officially recognised as conveying signs from heaven, and man was not ashamed of harbouring superstitions. The Jews of Palestine were very credulous. Some of them were willing to believe that Jesus was 'one of the old prophets risen from the dead', or even John the Baptist who had lately been beheaded. But it is a mistake to suppose that such miracles as the Virgin Birth and the Resurrection would have gained credence merely on the testimony of Mary the mother of Jesus or of Mary Magdalene; nor would the physical Resurrection have been regarded as proof of the divinity of Christ, since other examples of a return to life had been recorded. Those who assume—and there are many who do so, both among believers and among rationalists—that the Christian faith is built upon these miracles, and stands or falls with their factual occurrence, are behaving thoughtlessly. It was faith in Jesus that made them credible, not belief in their occurrence that created faith in Him. It was a common opinion that portents occur at the time of great events. 'When beggars die there are no comets seen.' Latin historians find room for stories such as 'bos in Etruria locutus' when the destiny of Rome was trembling in the balance. In Palestine a great teacher was expected to work miracles; they were part of his credentials. But since even in the documents which record so many mighty works done by Jesus He is reported to have protested against demands for a sign, we cannot suppose that His disciples were moved to leave all and follow Him as the result of thaumaturgic exhibitions, nor that the post-Resurrection appearances, so soon discontinued, turned the despair of the apostles to jubilant confidence. The disciples, like St. Paul, believed that their Master rose because they knew by inward experience that He was risen. His spiritual presence was a fact of which they could have no doubt. They believed in the literal inhabitation of good and evil spirits in the soul more simply than we

270

commonly do, though St. Paul's 'I, yet not I, but Christ liveth in me' expresses the deep conviction of thousands from that day to this.

For us, who do not expect portents to testify to spiritual truth, the miracles when taken out of their context have no religious value; regarded as abnormal occurrences they belong only to natural history. What we have to remember is that to very many minds even to-day they are so 'congruous' to the religious truths to which they testify that faith takes them under its wing. Those who so accept them do not really equate them with non-miraculous events in the natural order. They are such supernatural occurrences as might in their opinion be expected to accompany a unique revelation. It is certainly not my object to say anything to shake a connexion of ideas which seems to many much more than merely credible; but to regard these occurrences as the foundation of religious faith is, I am convinced, a disastrous mistake, since, as I have said, the miracles in themselves prove nothing that is of interest to religion.

The reluctance of the religious mind to

271

give them up is intelligible if we revert to my simile of a bridge. They have helped many to cross from the visible to the invisible world and back again. They have become, or perhaps they always were, symbols, myth, poetry; but symbols which are recognised as having only symbolic truth are no longer very helpful. They tend either to petrify or to evaporate, and either process is fatal to them. Those who cannot use the old symbols, which no longer help them to cross the gulf, must be allowed to use others, such as the metaphysical conceptions (themselves really symbolic) of appearance and reality, or of substance and shadow. 'Without a parable spake he not unto them.' 'Here we see by means of symbols, as in a mirror.'

It must, I think, be frankly admitted that much of the scaffolding of traditional Christianity has lost its evidential value. The argument from prophecy is being tacitly abandoned, for it is more than doubtful whether the gift of foretelling the future has ever been vouchsafed to human beings. The Old Testament prophets were forthtellers rather than foretellers. Those who foresaw the downfall of the Israelite monarchies showed no more than shrewd political insight. And as for miracle, we no longer expect that God will reveal Himself in this manner, and if we believe that He did so two thousand years ago, the substance of the revelation must carry the miracle, not the miracle the revelation. It is a peculiarity of theological architecture that the 'foundations' are ingeniously supported by the superstructure.

It is sometimes said that the Incarnation is a greater miracle than the Virgin Birth, and that those who think the evidence for the latter insufficient should logically be even more sceptical about the divinity of Christ. But the evidence for a unique spiritual revelation at this time is as cogent as any evidence can be. It can be disputed only by those who undervalue the content of the revelation, and on this we may perhaps say, *securus iudicat orbis terrarum*. We are not likely now to hear much of an objection which was sometimes raised when belief in continuous progress was a commonly received superstition, namely, that it is not likely that the supreme revelation was made nearly two thousand years ago. The thousand years between Buddha and Mohammed

saw the birth of all the great religions which
divide the allegiance of civilised mankind;
and if the art of sculpture culminated in
ancient Greece, and the art of painting in
Renaissance Italy, there is nothing unlikely
in the fact that the highest religion of the
Spirit appeared 'in the fullness of time'—i.e.
at the earliest possible moment—in the first
century, and in Palestine. The question to
which we are no longer prepared to give a
decided answer is whether such a revelation,
whether we call it unique or only supreme,
would probably be attended by portents in
the natural order. And we may fairly say
that a negative answer would not inflict a
mortal wound on our religious faith.

It is also important not to exaggerate the
abruptness or the novelty of the revelation
in the Person of Christ. It was prepared for
in the religious experience of the Jewish
nation, and, as Clement of Alexandria was
glad to recognise, in the long efforts of the
Greeks to discover ultimate truth. 'Those
who, like Heracleitus and Socrates, lived
under the guidance of the divine Logos, were
Christians before Christ.' Even St. Augustine has the remarkable statement that the

274

religion which is now called Christianity has always been in existence, though under other names. In the Epistle to Diognetus we read: 'This is He who was from the beginning, who appeared as new and was found to be old, and is ever being born young in the hearts of saints.' Modern theology, and not least in Protestant countries, has been more exclusive and less liberal than the early Fathers of the Church.

The words of the Johannine Christ, 'I have yet many things to say unto you, but ye cannot bear them now,' and the promise that the Paraclete will 'lead you into all truth', recognise fully that though the Incarnation was the beginning of a new dispensation, it was not the terminal phase of that revelation. If Catholicism has erred in confining the 'interpretation' of doctrine to the institutional Church, it has been an error of Protestantism to identify Christianity with a 'Jesus-worship' which Christ Himself would never have encouraged. '*Conversio fit ad Dominum ut Spiritum*', as Bengel wrote, quite in accordance with St. Paul. It is the heavenly and exalted Christ, immanent in the hearts of men, whom we worship. His office in the world is very far from being finished. We have only to be careful that we 'grow up into Him in all things', not out of Him into something alien from His Spirit.

There are other parts of the legacy of traditional Christianity which are falling into the background. It was early noticed that the writers of the Oxford Movement, both in its original form and still more in its revival under such men as Aubrey Moore and Charles Gore, laid much more stress on the Incarnation than on the Atonement. This change of emphasis, in my judgment, greatly strengthened the Christian position. For the Incarnation, as St. Augustine perceived, is the great addition which Christianity has made to the later Platonism, a school of thought to which the Church in all other ways owed so much. Not only was the Incarnation the central fact of history, but the whole world, seen from above, as it were, is incarnational, though not in equal degrees, not 'as full, as perfect, in a hair as heart.' Sacramental religion does not reject special means of grace; and we may perhaps mediate between the champions of 'faith' and 'works' by saying that the external life of a good

276

Christian is the sacrament, the outward visible sign of the inward spiritual grace by which 'Christ liveth in him'. We may follow Westcott in saying that the universe is the hymn of the Logos to the glory of God the Father. As compared with this thought, which is capable of covering the whole of our spiritual life, the old doctrine of the Atonement leaves us cold, and we do not find it easy to dissociate it from juridical ideas which seem unworthy of the God whom Christ revealed to us.

There is, however, one important point in which I think we must return to traditional theology. A Christianity which rejects the belief in evil spirits is not the religion of Christ or of the apostles or of the Catholic Church. The Devil, it has been said, has no better trick than to pretend to be dead, and Liberal theology has made a dangerous mistake in trying to eliminate him. The error is partly the result of the perfectibility heresy of the nineteenth century, partly of the very inadequate view of sin ('Dieu me pardonnera; c'est son métier') prevalent in our day, and partly of the same facile philosophical monism which has tried to solve ultimate

277

problems by putting matter inside mind, or mind inside matter. Evil, in the same way, must somehow be put inside good. It must somehow be supplemented and neutralised 'in the Absolute'. So Bradley argues, with much acceptance. He has got rid of the Devil; but in his system does the God of religion fare much better? It will not do. Evil is not negative but positive. For us finite beings it is as real as good. I know that for the Platonist 'Spirit (*Nous*) is sinless', and so, for Plotinus, is the higher soul; but as Iamblichus and Proclus, for once deserting their master, object, 'If the will can sin, how can the soul be sinless?' For the Christian, there may be 'defilement of the spirit' as well as of the flesh, and this implies that there is such a thing as 'spiritual wickedness in the heavenly places'. We cannot solve the terrible problem of evil by suppressing one side of it. No one has yet answered the cruel dilemma of St. Augustine: 'Either God cannot abolish evil, or He will not. If He will not, He is not good; if He cannot, He is not omnipotent.' To leave the matter there is a humiliation for a philosopher; for religion it is just a fact which we must recognise. If we

278

have to choose between recognising recent events as an outbreak of real Satanism, and repeating with Pope 'all partial evil universal good', I do not think we need hesitate to accept the former.

These questions are interesting mainly to theologians. But belief in a future life deeply concerns us all. The most startling change in Christian preaching is the almost total disappearance of references to future reward and punishment in sermons and religious literature. I am not acquainted with recent homiletic utterances either in the Roman Church or in some of the minor Protestant bodies; but in my own Church and in the most representative members of the Presbyterians and the Free Churches it would be true to say that the future life is seldom touched upon except as a state in which we may hope to be reunited to those whom we have loved on earth. Retributive future bliss and future torment are seldom mentioned; such sermons as those of Jonathan Edwards would drive almost any congregation out of doors.

Many even of the clergy repudiate the doctrine of eternal torment, though universalism is declared to be heretical in the Anglican Articles. The old doctrine is felt to be morally incredible, and so it is; but only half of it is rejected. Almost everyone, if he spoke his mind, would say, 'I know I don't deserve to go to heaven. I have done a great many things that I am very sorry for, and I have often forgotten my Maker. But I have tried to lead a decent life, and I really don't think I deserve to be roasted for all eternity.' No attempt to justify the classification of mankind into the saved and the damned can make the doctrine credible, if we believe in the justice of God. The parable of the sheep and the goats, which is not a description of the day of judgment, only emphasises that God will judge us according as we have obeyed or disobeyed the law of love; and the same is true of the parable of Dives and Lazarus.

Eschatology is and must be symbolic. Heaven and hell are not geographical expressions, nor is eternity a series of moments which for each of us has a beginning and no end. 'Eye hath not seen, nor ear heard, neither hath it entered into the heart of man to conceive' what the conditions of existence will be when 'there shall be time no longer'. A Buddhist sage says: 'Since all forms of existence are done away, all paths of speech are done away likewise.' If this were not so, the mass of contradictions in which Christian eschatology is involved by the attempt to combine Jewish belief in the resurrection of the flesh with Greek belief in the immortality of the soul would long ago have become intolerable. As far as I can see, we must be content with the following affirmations.

Everlastingness is the time-form of eternity, and while we live here we must be content to think of eternal life under this form, while admitting that it is only symbolic. Our rank in the scale of being is determined by the objects on which we set our hearts. Good and bad *mores*, as St. Augustine says, are the result of good and bad *amores*. What we are interested in, what we love, that we are. We have no right to assume that we shall be given a second chance, nor that there is any progress in eternity. Our choice, then, is of infinite importance to ourselves, and we can understand why popular teachers, addressing the ignorant and half-converted, drew their

pictures with the help of the most staring
colours in their paint-box. But God will not
cease to be just, and in dealing with such
poor creatures as we are, the highest justice
may be mercy. We are certainly not annihilated at death; as Lewis Nettleship was
fond of saying, 'Death does not count.' And
love, which is 'as strong as death', is not
extinguished either.

In the so-called ages of faith, when these
bribes and threats were freely uttered, and
often paid for in a very onerous tariff of
fire-insurance, was their effect on conduct
anything like what might have been expected? All the evidence goes to show that it
was not. The violence and brutality of the
dark and earlier middle ages were almost
incredible. The Penitentiaries give us the
impression of a population sunk in bestial
vice as well as crime. At a time when the
Church exalted the virtue of chastity to what
seems to us a disproportionate eminence,
writers like Boccaccio almost rival Petronius
in obscenity. We can hardly doubt that these
sanctions were never really quite believed in
by the irreligious; many of the saints frankly
disliked them, and wished that they might

282

be allowed to love God for Himself alone. We therefore need not be surprised that the modern reluctance to make these appeals has not been accompanied by any obvious deterioration in private morality. That States have trampled on every law, human and divine, is too true; but this can hardly be the result of a change in belief about the future life; for 'a corporation has neither a body to be kicked nor a soul to be damned.'

'Reduced Christianity!' the traditionalists will say. But is not the original Gospel a simple matter—till we try to practise it? It did not go much beyond the summary of the prophet Micah. 'Wherewith shall I come before the Lord, and bow myself before the high God? Shall I come before Him with burnt offerings, with calves of a year old? Will the Lord be pleased with thousands of rams, and ten thousands of rivers of oil? Shall I give my first-born for my transgressions, the fruit of my body for the sin of my soul? He hath showed thee, O man, what is good; and what doth the Lord require of thee, but to do justly and to love mercy, and to walk humbly with thy God?' We are not obliged to be more orthodox than Christ.

Faith is not merely a matter of emotion, nor of the will. It requires an intellectual justification; and is this forthcoming? If the external props which we have mentioned are insufficient, are we thrown back on what is variously called the inner light, mystical experience, and the testimony of the Holy Spirit? Is this enough?

The Roman Church says that it is not enough. We have no immediate apprehension of God which dispenses us from the exercise of thought and from an act of faith. This error their theologians call ontologism. It may be found in Jacobi, and in the American Theodore Parker. The Roman doctrine is that, in the words of a Papal decree of 1855, 'rational conclusions can prove with certainty the existence of God, the spiritual nature of the soul, and the freedom of the will.' The Vatican Council of 1870 anathematises those who say that the true God cannot be known by the certain light of natural reason. This belief is a valid inference founded on certain classical proofs or arguments, which are discussed at length in many easily accessible books.

The first, the ontological proof, is not used

by St. Thomas Aquinas nor by his modern disciples. It had been stated in a form the fallacy of which is apparent even to a child; Kant had no difficulty in dismissing it. But the real strength of the argument is expressed in a famous saying of Aquinas himself: '*impossibile est naturale desiderium esse inane*'—'it is impossible that any natural need should be vain.' It would be, not strictly impossible, but 'intolerable', as Lotze says, to suppose that our highest aspirations are in a conspiracy to deceive us. It is therefore a reasonable act of faith to believe that the object of religious worship, and of the yearning love of the mystic, has an existence outside the imagination of the believer.

Of the cosmological and teleological 'proofs' it is enough here to say that they are in favour of theism, but do not bring us all the way to the God of religion. The evidence for a mind in the natural order seems to me overwhelming; but this argument cannot prove that the mind in creation is either omnipotent or what we call good. The fourth, the moral argument, is on a different footing, since goodness is one of the ultimate values in which the nature of God is revealed to us. The 'ought' is the voice of the super-personal spirit within us.

Thomism is distrustful of mysticism, and modern Thomists do not make much use of the inner light, which ecclesiastics mistrust as an independent and sometimes rebellious source of individual inspiration. But when St. Thomas says that the Holy Spirit is present in the human soul 'in His *substance*', he concedes enough to satisfy Eckhart himself. It is recorded of him that he laid down his pen, leaving his work unfinished, because he had 'seen' what made books seem superfluous.

The validity of the argument from mystical experiences depends on the Platonic and Christian belief that progress in the spiritual life and knowledge of God proceed *pari passu*. If we live as we ought, we shall see things as they are, and if we see things as they are, we shall live as we ought. The path of ascent begins with faith, which Clement of Alexandria defines as 'compendious knowledge'. Faith is the resolution to stand or fall by the noblest hypothesis. The earnest endeavour to purify the character sets free the highest activity of the soul, *Nous* or

Pneuma, and enables it to come in contact with reality as it is. So Faith passes into Knowledge, and, as Plato says, 'the fully real is fully knowable.' Lastly, love takes the soul in hand, and unites knower and known in unity. This is the mystic's path, which ends in the beatific vision. But even at the earlier stages faith, though it sees through a glass darkly, can 'see the invisible' (Hebrews, v. 27). St. Augustine's comment is, *Errabant quidem adhuc et patriam quaerebant, sed duce Christo errare non poterant. Via illis erat visio Dei.*' ('They were still wandering and seeking their country, but with Christ as their guide they could not go astray. Their journey was the vision of God.') '*Fides quaerit, intellectus invenit,*' he says elsewhere.

There is not necessarily anything of what is vulgarly supposed to be meant by mysticism in this scheme; no ecstasy, no swooning into the Absolute, no dark night of the soul. It rests on the belief that the truths of religion, being spiritual, are spiritually discerned. The natural man cannot know them, because he is blind to the eternal values which can be seen only by the pure in heart. Those who have trodden the path have not the slightest doubt about the reality of what they have seen; and when we allow for the extreme difficulty of putting such experiences into words, their witness agrees together.

Ought we to identify the higher philosophy—philosophy as the *ars vitae*—with the higher religion, or with others ought we to say that philosophy is the higher form of which religion is the lower? There is this great difference, that religion begins with God, God imperfectly known but confidently believed to exist, while philosophy finds Him at the culminating point of its enquiry. The intercourse between the soul of the religious man and God is from first to last an 'I' and 'Thou' relationship; for the philosopher God remains to the last 'He' or 'It'. In the twentieth and last of a typical series of Gifford Lectures He may proclaim Himself ready to 'emerge'.

The question may here be raised. If God reveals Himself to man as perfect truth, goodness, and beauty, are not these the attributes of an impersonal Being? If we cannot pray to a 'valid inference', no more can we pray to a triad of ultimate values. The answer is, I think, to be found in the famous words 'God is Love'. In every other experience, when we are brought near to the presence of God, we see but the fringes of His ways, and hear but a whisper of His voice. But love is the hierophant of the higher mysteries; it admits us into the actual presence of our Maker. This experience is possible when we have established an 'I' and 'Thou' relationship. If we cannot ourselves say with any confidence, 'I love God', thousands who have a right to speak can say so. And our experience of human love is enough to teach us what love is and may be. For Christ, whether we think of the historical Jesus or of His spiritual presence, it is easy to feel love, and 'he who hath seen Me hath seen the Father.' If He came into the room, should we not all fall on our knees?

This brief sketch of my own convictions may be enough to show what, in my opinion, the essentials of Christianity are. We have no right to expect that it will ever be the religion of the majority. Strait is the gate and narrow is the way that leadeth unto life, and few there be that find it. But neither have we any right to fear that it will decay or become extinct. There have been times when the Church was much more in the public eye, and much more powerful, than it is now. But this has always been the result of the unholy alliances which institutional religion is too ready to make. The times when the Church has been politically strongest have been notorious for scandals; the history of the Papacy in the 'ages of faith' is an astonishing record of vice, crime, and perfidy. Nor, as I have said, were those times distinguished by superior purity, justice, or humanity.

But we need not suppose that the inner light shines with equal brightness at all times. It seems to be true that periods of great brilliance and prosperity in secular civilisation have not been favourable to religion. The fifth century before Christ produced not only Pheidias and the great tragedians, but the cynical repudiation of all moral restraint upon cruelty and treachery which Thucydides describes. Philosophy was beginning to be religious in Plato; in Stoicism the alliance was ratified; but by this time the flowering time of Hellenic civilisation was over. The Hellenistic world turned to religion in the time of troubles; the century of Origen and

290

Plotinus was barren of secular culture except in jurisprudence. When the Renaissance was at its height, Italy was almost completely paganised, and there was a revival of cruelty and treachery which recalls Greece two thousand years before. Again in the nineteenth century, which posterity will recognise as a time of real progress and unique achievement in many fields, though society was kept outwardly respectable by the traditional puritanism of the dominant middle class, the religion of the Spirit was under a cloud, and the public conscience has not been strong enough to prevent the hideous outbreak of Satanism which now poisons and darkens Europe. There will and must be a religious revival, but we cannot be sure when it will come nor what form it will take.

Educated people hope for an Erasmian reformation, which will relegate to the sphere of pious opinion some traditional doctrines which have lost their symbolic value, and which are a heavy burden upon many who can only retain their loyalty to the Church at the price of disloyalty to their intellectual integrity. Thanks to the courage of a small number of men who were not afraid of being ostracised as heretics in their day, a large measure of freedom has been gained in the Church of England and in some of the Free Churches. But ecclesiastical authority has to be guided by the wishes of the minority who still go to church, not of the majority who stop away. The alienation from institutional religion has gone so far that it may be too late to make the accommodations necessary to heal the breach between dogmatic Christianity and secular knowledge.

The issue however is not so clearly defined as it seemed to be in the last century, when 'agnostics' were so very sure of the boundary line between realities and dreams, between the solid facts which could be measured and counted, and the luminous haze of imaginary values which floated ineffectively over the only real world. 'Science' is no longer so confident, and no longer speaks with one voice. Biologists, as I have said, are still, with notable exceptions, content with the materialistic standpoint of the nineteenth century, but astronomers and physicists are favourably disposed to theism, as indeed some of them were in the Victorian age, and some mathematicians would even be glad to be relieved of hampering entanglements with concrete facts.

The popular irrationalism in philosophy is all on the side of conservatism in dogma. If religion is a matter of the will and emotions, we may say with Pascal that the heart has its reasons which the intellect knows not of. Against this line of defence the Catholic theologians, to their honour, are waging a vigorous polemic.

When writing on this subject twenty years ago I expressed a fear that traditionalism in ethics was, in certain points, causing the Churches to be stranded in a backwater. Some of the new duties which the advance of science has brought home to the lay conscience were not acknowledged by ecclesiastical authority. A moral revolt, I said rightly, would be an extremely serious matter for organised Christianity. I did not mention the new liberty which is being claimed in matters of sex, because I thought and still think that this is an evil thing. Popular fiction, which tries to mirror, and really affects, the point of view of the younger generation, gives to sex far more importance

293

than it actually has in a decent and well-ordered life. I am confident that these now popular novels will soon be unreadable, not only as bad morality but as bad art. The two examples of new duties which I mentioned were the treatment of the lower animals and our duties to posterity.

As regards the former, the Protestant Churches, if not in the forefront of the campaign against cruel sports and fashions, are not obstructive. They disclaim any sympathy with the view which is traditional in the Roman Church, that the lower animals, since they have no souls, cannot be the subject of duties.

As regards the latter, I was and still am a keen eugenist. But, as usually happens, more intense research has made the laws of heredity seem more complicated. A few genuine scientists like Jennings in America throw cold water on the hopes of eugenists to improve the breed of mankind, or to arrest its deterioration, either by legislation or by voluntarily accepted principles of action. Others, most unfairly on the whole, have suspected eugenists of assuming that financially successful families are biologically superior to the unpropertied masses. The compulsory mutilation of thousands of persons in Nazi Germany has not made negative eugenics more popular. In the last few years the depopulation scare, of which I have spoken in another place, has to some extent diverted the attention of the Eugenics Society from the subjects which formerly engaged its attention. The most important change in the last twenty years has been the acceptance of family limitation as a legitimate act.

The future of the Churches is much more precarious than that of Christianity. The parochial machinery is out of date. The Anglican liturgies need more drastic revision than was attempted in the abortive new prayer book of 1928. Our services are overweighted with the Jewish scriptures. The sermon is no longer, if it ever was, an intellectual stimulus for a public which possessed few books. We sometimes forget how little of all this machinery is needed in the East, where religions grow wild. And there is some danger that we may be keeping our gardeners in hothouses, while the young plants are in the open air.

A useful change, I think, would be to put all candidates for Holy Orders through a course of the psychology of religion, with a view to making them trained consultants for those who are in trouble with their souls. Most of us, at one time or another, would be glad of spiritual counsel if we knew where to find it. Perhaps half of the cases which would come before the consulting physician of the soul would have some connection with sex, a subject on which useful training is quite possible, and is now very seldom given. The parish priest ought to be qualified to deal with ordinary cases; the more difficult or complicated could be referred to a specialist, who should be acquainted with the methods of such institutions as the Tavistock Clinic. The clergyman of the future will be first and foremost a physician of the soul.

Christianity, if we may say so with all reverence, was a religion founded by a layman for laymen. The first apostles included fishermen, two men with Greek names, a tax-gatherer, an ex-communist—Simon Zelotes, but no priests. Nothing was further from the mind of Christ than to found a totalitarian Church. It is useless for a Chris-

tian to accept St. Paul's words, 'in Christ
there is neither Jew nor Greek, barbarian,
Scythian, bond nor free,' unless he is prepared to add, 'In Christ there is neither
Catholic nor Protestant, neither Churchman
nor Dissenter, neither orthodox nor heretic.'
'The humble, meek, merciful, just, pious,
and devout souls,' says William Penn, 'are
everywhere of one religion; and when death
has taken off the mask they will know one
another, though the divers liveries they wear
here make them strangers.' 'By their fruits
ye shall know them.' 'If any man have not
the spirit of Christ, he is none of His.' The
fruits of theological controversy are bitter
and divisive; the fruits of the Spirit, love,
joy, peace, long-suffering, gentleness, goodness, faith, meekness, patience, unite men
of good will and bring into one flock those
who can never be cooped in one fold.
Is it not instructive to find Gregory of
Nazianzus, who had actually presided at the
Ecumenical Council of 381, writing to Pro-
copius the Prefect of Constantinople, 'My
own inclination is to avoid all assemblies of
bishops, for I have never seen any Council
come to a good end, nor solve any evils? It

usually increases them. You always find there love of contention and love of power.' Hilary of Poitiers in 360 writes: 'Since Nicaea we have done nothing but compose creeds. Every year we make new creeds and define invisible mysteries. . . . Tearing one another to pieces we have been the cause of one another's ruin.'

The only apostolical succession has been in the lives of the saints. 'The one really formidable argument against the truth of the Christian religion', says Canon Barry almost audaciously, 'is the record of the Christian Church.' St. Paul knows of no other 'foundation' of the Church, no other 'Rock', than Christ Himself. The prerogative of Peter, like his 'bishopric' of Rome, was unknown till after his death.

The church, which consists of all 'who love the Lord Jesus Christ in uncorruptness' is a fountain of living water, not a cistern filled long ago; it is not condemned to live on its capital.

We crave for certainty, and certainty is ours, if we will earn it by seeking earnestly the pearl of great price. As even the Stoic Manilius says:

*Quid caelo dabimus? Quantum est quo
    veneat omne?*
*Impendendus homo est, Deus esse ut possit
    in ipso.*'[1]

As F. H. Bradley, no champion of orthodoxy, says: 'There is nothing more real than
what comes in religion. The man who demands a reality more solid than that of the
religious consciousness knows not what he
seeks.'

But certainty must be earned. A disciple
came to Junayd, the Sufi mystic, and said to
him, 'I am told that you possess the pearl of
divine knowledge; give it to me or sell it to
me.' Junayd answered, 'I cannot sell it, for
you have not the price of it. If I give it you,
you will have gained it too cheaply. You do
not know its value.' The unearned certainty
offered by Catholicism is spurious metal.
They appeal to the Vincentian canon, '*Quod
semper, quod ubique, quod ab omnibus.*'
'*Quod semper*' means in 1563: '*quod ubique*'
means at Trent; '*quod ab omnibus*' means by
a majority. No man may deliver his brother,

[1] 'What shall we give for heaven? At what price is the
All sold? A man must spend himself, that God may be
able to be in him.'

nor make agreement unto God for him. We must work out our own salvation with fear and trembling.

It would, I am sure, greatly strengthen the position of Christianity if we could be content to accept as essential what was enough to bring the original disciples to Christ, and to leave it free to our contemporaries either to take shelter beneath the traditional edifice of dogma or to choose other symbols more in harmony with their own ways of thought. The ancient creeds, which were compiled in the way we have seen, not at all the best way, as many of those who helped to draw them up admitted, are very far from being satisfactory statements of our living faith. They are like tattered banners hung round the walls of our churches. Attempts have been made to tabulate shorter and simpler summaries of Christian belief, taken entirely from the words of the New Testament. An example of these, by the late Sir Arnold Wilson, was printed in the *Spectator* for December 9th, 1932.

'God is Spirit; and they that worship Him must worship Him in spirit and in truth. God is light; and if we walk in the light as

300

He is in the light we have fellowship one with another. God is love; and everyone that loveth is born of God and knoweth God. Jesus is the Son of God; and God hath given to us eternal life, and this life is in His Son. We are children of God; and He hath given us of His Spirit. If we confess our sins He is faithful and just to forgive us our sins. The world passeth away and the lust thereof; but he that doeth the will of God abideth for ever. Amen.'

Those who are content with this creed should not feel themselves excluded from the service of the Church.

PRINTED IN GREAT BRITAIN
BY ROBERT MACLEHOSE AND CO. LTD
THE UNIVERSITY PRESS, GLASGOW